Alcohol

ISSUES
(formerly Issues for the Nineties)

Volume 39

Editor

Craig Donnellan

Independence
Educational Publishers
Cambridge

First published by Independence
PO Box 295
Cambridge CB1 3XP
England

British Library Cataloguing in Publication Data
Alcohol – (Issues Series)
I. Donnellan, Craig II. Series
362.2'92

ISBN 1 86168 081 3

Printed in Great Britain
City Print Ltd
Milton Keynes

Typeset by
Claire Boyd

Cover
The illustration on the front cover is by
Pumpkin House.

CONTENTS

Introduction

Alcohol is the thirty-ninth volume in the series: **Issues**. The aim of this series is to offer up-to-date information about important issues in our world.

Alcohol looks at the impact of alcohol on society.

The information comes from a wide variety of sources and includes:
Government reports and statistics
Newspaper reports and features
Magazine articles and surveys
Literature from lobby groups
and charitable organisations.

It is hoped that, as you read about the many aspects of the issues explored in this book, you will critically evaluate the information presented. It is important that you decide whether you are being presented with facts or opinions. Does the writer give a biased or an unbiased report? If an opinion is being expressed, do you agree with the writer?

Alcohol offers a useful starting-point for those who need convenient access to information about the many issues involved. However, it is only a starting-point. At the back of the book is a list of organisations which you may want to contact for further information.

*****

Alcohol

Information from the Institute for the Study of Drug Dependency (ISDD)

Alcohol consists mainly of ethanol and water. Beer contains 1 part ethanol to every 20 parts water, wine 1 in 8 and some spirits 1 in 2.

Alcohol depresses your nervous system within 5 to 10 minutes of drinking it, making you feel relaxed and less inhibited. Larger doses get you drunk, causing disorientation, slurred speech, exaggerated moods and nausea. Your mood at the time of drinking will almost always impact on how alcohol will affect you. Drinking also affects your ability to drive and operate machinery, even the morning after. Amounts needed to get you drunk vary depending on your size, gender, metabolism, whether you have an empty stomach or not and on your tolerance, i.e. how used you are to alcohol.

Alcohol is the most commonly available and accepted form of intoxication. At college or university, alcohol can be a mainstay of social life. Drinking and having fun at college may seem at times one and the same thing. This may be your first encounter with getting drunk, or your first time getting drunk so badly, so often, and so readily.

Many of you who will be experimenting with alcohol should note that drinking patterns for the rest of your life can be set during your time at college or university.

You may, because of your religion or just through preference, not like drinking or getting drunk. If this is you, the focus on drink for socialising at college can cause frustration and isolation. There are other ways, luckily, of meeting people through, for example, many of the college clubs and activities groups. Attitudes at many pubs and cafes are changing and non-alcoholic drinks are becoming more available and more acceptable. If your student union bar only sells a limited range of non-alcoholic drinks or only promotes alcoholic drinks, make people listen by complaining to the student union or the catering management. Request appreciation for non-alcohol drinkers.

The morning after

The hangover is the body's reaction to breaking down the alcohol consumed the day or night before. Symptoms include headache (caused by dehydration), tiredness, and an upset or raw stomach. Preventing dehydration will go a long way towards staving off the effects of a hangover. Replenishing the body's sugar and salt levels will speed up the recovery. Drink plenty of water before dozing off or as much as you can the next day. Try eating some light food if you can. Avoid tea or coffee as they tend to dehydrate your body. Clean water or isotonic drinks are best.

Your mood too will be generally low and your stamina and mental ability will be diminished, so avoid strenuous activity. Try planning your drinking around times that will not disrupt other activities and college work.

After a heavy session the night before, remember that you may still have a lot of alcohol in your system and therefore could still be drunk. Many motorists have been convicted of drink-driving when breathalysed the next morning following a night out.

Drinking alcohol a lot

Drinking a lot at college is fairly common. As with all drugs, people can come to rely on its effects when going out or when having a good time. Tolerance can build up, requiring more and more drink to get the same effects. Regular drinking can affect your daily health, causing liver damage and considerable weight gain. Drinks are very high in calories – some pints of beer have the same amount of calories as a Mars bar. In extreme cases heavy drinking can cause heart disease and even brain damage. More common

problems include unsafe sex, getting involved in accidents and acts of violence.

How much is too much?

A lot has been said about 'safe limits'. Government guidelines advise safe limits of 3-4 units per day for men and 2-3 for women (a pint of normal lager is 2 units and a single whisky 1 unit). These levels have proven difficult to grasp and not applicable to all individuals. On the whole they don't reflect the drinking habits of young people.

Abstaining from drinking only to make up for it later in a binge or bender is one example of how these guidelines can be misinterpreted and used unsafely. It is best to judge each time you go out, what the appropriate amount should be and try sticking to it. Think about what you are doing later or the next day. A little bit of planning may save you and others a lot of bother.

Mixing with other drugs

Drinking a lot by itself can be a problem, but if alcohol is taken at the same time as other drugs that depress your system, the effects of both will be exaggerated and can prove dangerous. Overdose is a real danger if alcohol is mixed with strong depressants such as methadone, heroin, Valium or temazepam. Vomiting whilst unconscious is a common cause of death.

Taking stimulants with alcohol can also cause problems. Not only will these drugs work against each

other, the strain on the body and heart can also cause damage and make you feel ill. Taking alcohol with ecstasy can, for example, distort the effects of the ecstasy and dehydrate your body making you feel weak and edgy.

Keep ahead

As well as the general guidelines:
- Avoid mixing with other drugs, especially strong downers such as methadone, heroin, GHB tranquillisers and other prescription drugs – in particular antihistamines and certain types of antidepressants.
- Avoid mixing with ecstasy or speed in hot clubs – drink water or soft drinks to prevent dehydration.

- Don't drink and drive, and be careful the morning after – you could still be drunk from the night before.
- Try to keep your water levels up by drinking some water or a soft drink every so often.
- Try having something to eat before you start drinking.
- Make plans before you start drinking about how to get home properly. Without them, you may be tempted to drive home drunk.

• The above information is from the Institute for the Study of Drug Dependency (ISDD) web site. See page 43 for details.

© Institute for the Study of Drug Dependency (ISDD)

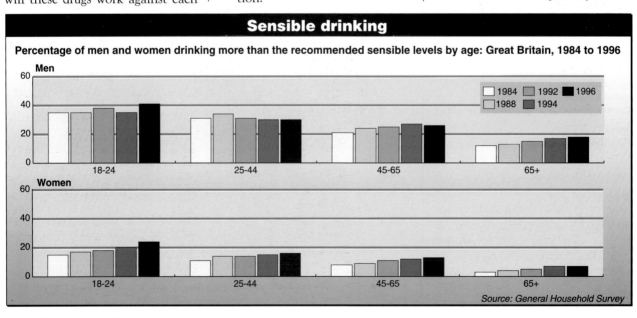

Sensible drinking

Percentage of men and women drinking more than the recommended sensible levels by age: Great Britain, 1984 to 1996

Men

Legend: 1984, 1988, 1992, 1994, 1996

Women

Source: General Household Survey

Alcohol and the law

Information from Alcohol Concern

The laws governing the consumption, sale and use of alcohol are extremely complex. This is a summary of the main points and should not be take as a definitive statement.

Licensed premises

The sale of alcohol has been regulated for centuries, with the aim of ensuring that it is not sold without prior permission.

In England and Wales, the Licensing Act 1964 is the main control over where, when and to whom alcohol can be sold. It is administered by licensing justices. They have discretion to grant a licence to sell alcohol to any person they think 'fit and proper'. Licences can be for consumption either on or off the premises and it is an offence to retail alcohol without a licence. An opportunity is provided for anyone (including the police and local residents) to object to the renewal of a licence on a wide variety of grounds.

In Scotland, the main control is the Licensing (Scotland) Act 1976. A similar system of licensing operates, under the control of licensing boards.

Licensing hours

(England and Wales) – Weekdays excluding Christmas Day[1]
On-licences
11am to 11pm
Off-licences
8am to 11pm

Sundays excluding Christmas Day[2]
On-licences
12 noon to 10.30pm
Off-licences
10am to 10.30pm

Christmas Day
On-licences
12 noon to 3pm and 7pm to 10.30pm

Different hours apply to registered clubs, and to premises with Special Hours Certificates, Supper Hours Certificates or Restaurant Licences.

Laws governing purchase and consumption of alcohol by young people

Under 5 – May not be given alcohol except on medical orders. Law: Children and Young Persons Act, 1933
5+ – May consume alcohol e.g. at home, in registered clubs. It is only illegal for those aged 5-18 to drink alcohol on licensed premises.
Under 14 – May not be present in the bar of licensed premises unless accompanied by a person over 18, it is before 9pm and a children's certificate relating to the bar is in force. Law: Licensing Act 1964.
14 and over – May be in the bar of licensed premises during permitted hours, at licensee's discretion. Law: Licensing Act 1964 and Deregulation and Contracting Out Act 1994.
Under 16 – May be present in a restaurant etc where alcohol is served with a meal and at the licensee's discretion may consume (but not purchase) alcohol bought by an accompanying adult (parent or guardian).
16 and over – May purchase beer, porter, cider or perry with a meal in an eating area on licensed premises. In Scotland wine can also be bought. Law: Licensing Act 1964
Under 18 – May not purchase or be supplied with or consume alcohol in a bar. Law: Licensing Act 1964.

Police have powers to confiscate alcohol from under-18s drinking in public and to contact their parents. Law: Confiscation of Alcohol (Young Persons) Act 1997.

In Northern Ireland only, may not enter licensed premises. Law: Licensing Act 1964. May not be employed in a bar of licensed premises. Law: Licensing Act 1964.
16-18 – unless as part of Modern Apprenticeship Scheme
Any age – may be present in registered private members' clubs

Drunkenness

There are many laws, some going back to the nineteenth century, governing drunken behaviour:

1839 Metropolitan Police Act
Offence – Being drunk in a street or public place in the Metropolitan Police area and being guilty of riotous or indecent behaviour

1872 Licensing Act
Offence – Being drunk in a highway or other public place or on licensed premises

1902 Licensing Act
Offences
1) being drunk in charge of a child under 7
2) being drunk and incapable on any highway or other public place

1903 Licensing (Scotland) Act
Offence – Being drunk and incapable

1964 Licensing Act
Offences
1) offence for licensee to permit drunkenness on premises and to serve a drunken customer
2) offence of procuring a drink for a drunken person and of aiding a drunken person to obtain or consume alcohol in licensed premises
3) licensees given powers to refuse to admit to, or expel from, licensed premises any drunken person

1967 Criminal Justice Act
Offence – Increased the penalty for drunk and disorderly offences

1980 Criminal Justice (Scotland) Act
Offence – Increased the penalty for drunkenness offences in Scotland

1980 Licensed Premises (Exclusion of Certain Persons) Act
Offence – Any person convicted of any offence committed in licensed premises involving violence may be banned from entering licensed premises

1985 Sporting Events (Control of Alcohol) Act
Offence – Prohibits the possession of alcohol at specific sporting events, and on public transport

vehicles travelling to and from these events.

Local bye-laws
May prohibit drinking in designated areas

Drink/driving laws

The police can ask someone to be tested if they have reasonable cause to suspect:
- the person has been driving (or attempting to drive) with alcohol in their body
- that a moving traffic offence has been committed
- that the person has been involved in an accident

The prescribed limits are
- 35 micrograms of alcohol in 100 millilitres of breath
- 80 milligrams of alcohol in 100 ml of blood.
- 107 milligrams of alcohol per 100 ml of urine.[3]

Causing death by careless driving whilst under the influence of drink or drugs[3]
Penalty – 10 years' imprisonment and a disqualification of at least 2 years

Driving or attempting to drive whilst above the legal limit or unfit through drink[4]
Penalty – 6 months' imprisonment plus a fine of £5,000 and a disqualification of at least 12 months (3 years if convicted twice in 10 years)

In charge of a vehicle whilst above the legal limit or unfit through drink[4]
Penalty – 3 months' imprisonment plus a fine of £2,500 and a disqualification

Refusing to provide a specimen[4]
Penalty – 6 months' imprisonment plus a fine of £5,000 and a disqualification of at least 12 months

High-risk offenders

High-risk offenders are those who
- refuse to provide a specimen
- are convicted at two and a half times the legal limit
- are convicted twice in ten years
  In all these cases an approved doctor has to certify that the person does not have a drink problem before the licence can be returned.
  The 1991 Road Traffic Act provided for an experiment in the rehabilitation of drink/drive offenders. Magistrates now have the power to send offenders on alcohol education courses that have been set up in a number of centres around the country. The evaluation of this scheme will continue until 1999.

Other forms of transport

The Transport and Works Act 1992 is concerned with the safety of railways and created a number of new offences aimed at railway staff who go to work under the influence of alcohol or drugs. They largely mirror the offences contained in the Road Traffic Act 1988, relating to driving or being in charge of a vehicle under the influence of drink or drugs.
They apply to a much wider range of individuals, from drivers and guards to track repairers.

References
1. Licensing Act 1988
2. Licensing (Sunday Hours) Act 1995
3. Road Traffic Act 1991
4. Road Traffic Act 1988

- The above is an extract from the Alcohol Concern web site. See page 43 for details

© Alcohol Concern

Facts about alcohol

Information from LifeLine

- Alcohol reaches the brain within five minutes of being swallowed.
- Alcohol is a depressant drug that slows down the activity of the brain.
- Eating before drinking slows down the rate at which alcohol has its effects.
- Fizzy drinks increase the speed at which alcohol is absorbed into the body.
- Alcohol affects women more quickly than it does men and the effects last longer.
- Young people tend to be lighter than adults. The lighter your body weight the greater the effects of alcohol.
- There is no safe limit for drinking and driving. Even at the legal limit young drivers are five times more likely to have an accident than non-drinkers.
- Alcohol affects our sense of right or wrong before it affects our co-ordination.
- Underage drinking starts young, nearly 90% of boys in England have drunk alcohol by the age of 13.
- Around 25% of 13-17-year-olds get into arguments or fights after drinking alcohol.
- One thousand children aged under 15 are admitted to hospital each year with acute alcohol poisoning. All of these need emergency treatment and may end up in intensive care.
- 18-24-year-olds are the heaviest drinkers in the population.
- Men who drink regularly at unsafe levels risk impotence and infertility.
- Men say that drinking makes them feel sexy. Women on the whole do not agree. Most women think that men who drink too much are embarrassing and dangerous.
- Alcohol is loaded with calories so it can make you fat.
- People who drink too much in an evening may still be over the legal limit for driving the next morning.
- It takes the liver one hour to break down one unit of alcohol.
- There is only one cure for a hangover – TIME! NOTHING else works!!
- People who use alcohol early in their lives are more likely to use illegal drugs.

- The above is an extract from *The Big Blue Book of Booze*, produced by LifeLine. See page 41 for address details.

© Lifeline

Intoxicating facts

Information from the Health Education Authority (HEA)

In 41 per cent of all 'contact crime' the victim said the offender had been drinking alcohol. This included 32 per cent of incidents of domestic violence, 17 per cent of muggings, 53 per cent of incidents of violence by a stranger and 45 per cent of incidents by an acquaintance.

The 1996 British Crime Survey England and Wales. *Home Office Statistical Bulletin* Issue 19/96

A third of assaults by a stranger and a fifth of assaults by an acquaintance take place in or around a pub, club or other licensed premises. In the case of violence by a stranger, a glass or bottle was the most commonly used weapon.

The 1996 British Crime Survey

A Finnish study found that men who binge on beer (six or more bottles in a session) have a much higher risk of early death, regardless of their total average consumption. Other risks also increased, including injuries, poisoning, violence and suicide.

Kauhanen et al, Beer bingeing and mortality, *BMJ* October 1997

About a quarter of all alcohol-related deaths are due to accidents.

Analysis of mortality data for 1995, quoted in *Sensible Drinking*. The Report of an Inter-Departmental Working Group. Department of Health 1995.

About half of all pedestrians aged 16-60 killed in road traffic accidents had more alcohol in their bloodstream than the legal drink-drive limit.

Dept of Transport. *The involvement of alcohol in fatal accidents to adult pedestrians.* Report No. 343. Transport Research Laboratory, 1992

Half of all adults admitted to hospital surgical units with head injuries are drunk.

Williams RJLI et al. Resource Implications of head injuries on an acute surgical unit. *JR Soc Med,* 1994; 87: 83-6

Alcohol was reported as a factor in at least 7 per cent of accidental drownings in 1994.

Office for National Statistics, personal communication, 1996

Violence is now the leading cause of facial injuries in Britain – until the late 1980s it was road traffic accidents.

Policing Today, Vol 3 Issue 2, June 1997

15,789 people in England and Wales were found guilty of offences of drunkenness in 1995. Police formally cautioned a further 22,809. The ratio of men to women was 10:1.

Home Office, 1997

Tips to survive the party season

With the party season looming, many people may feel under pressure to drink a lot more than usual simply because it's what's expected. And for people who don't have a flood of party invites, the run-up to Christmas can be a lonely, depressing time and alcohol may seem to be one way of coping. Whatever your circumstances, the following are a few tips which might help you to stay in control and still have a good time.

- Work out and stick to a limit for any day and for special occasions
- Don't let people pressure you into having another drink – it's ok to say no
- Skip rounds, or choose an alcohol-free drink during some of them
- Pace yourself – or choose smaller drinks, a half instead of a pint
- Have days when you don't drink at all
- Watch it at home – most people pour much larger drinks than they get in a pub
- Try to find other ways to relax
- Don't drink on an empty stomach – and try to eat something during the evening

If you do overdo it, it's a good idea to lay off alcohol for 48 hours to give your body time to recover.

There are lots of real benefits from not overdoing it. Some of these include:
- More energy – drinking disturbs your sleep and can leave you feeling worn out
- A new sense of feeling in control
- Improved concentration and a clear head
- More money
- More pleasure out of your sex life
- Your skin will be healthier and you'll be less likely to put on weight
- Fewer hangovers, headaches and stomach upsets
- Fewer arguments and rows
- Less risk of an accident
- Less vulnerability – being drunk can put you at risk of opportunistic crime.

© Health Education Authority (HEA)

Booze: Britain's real drug crisis

When a teenager dies after taking Ecstasy it's front-page news. The Government now warns us of a new heroin epidemic. But a far more deadly and acceptable substance is freely available at a bar, restaurant or supermarket near you. By Suzanne Moore

I walked into the smoke-filled room and breathed a sigh of relief. It was obvious that I could get what I was looking for. Scoring is never difficult in places like this and it was obvious that I could not only get my drug of choice, but I could get it in any combination I desired. The dealers were polite enough, and even offered to bring it over to the table. I remembered the first time I had indulged. It used to make me sick, but over the years I had built up a tolerance. Anyway, this was a drug I could handle; it made me feel better, more sociable; gave me a bit of a glow.

I don't have a habit. Of course not. What I do is entirely legal. My name is Suzanne and I am not an alcoholic. I just like a drink now and again. A lot of us do, and a lot of us are drinking far more than ever before. A lot more are dying as a result of it, but you wouldn't know that from reading the headlines of the last few days.

Illegal drugs are always far more newsworthy than legal ones and last week has not been a good week for the parents of teenage children. I sat watching the news with my teenage daughter while we were told that the country is on the brink of a second heroin epidemic. Heroin, like any other commodity with an image problem, has now been successfully rebranded. Freed from its association with dirty, middle-aged junkies, it is now offered to teenagers, even middle-class ones, in £5 wraps as a chill-out drug. The Police Research Group said: 'The Nineties have been dominated by the extensive use of drugs, like cannabis, amphetamines, and ecstasy, particularly by youth populations'.

The newsreader solemnly informed us of the signs of a teenage heroin user. They become listless, unresponsive and glassy-eyed and spend a lot of time in their rooms.

'Are you a heroin addict?' I asked my daughter, because as far as I can see these are merely the symptoms of adolescence. She made that noise that teenagers make when they consider their parents to be an utter embarrassment, and went up to her room.

By the middle of the week, however, the death of 18-year-old Julia Dawes had reminded us that other drugs besides heroin kill our children. 'Ecstasy kills teenage fitness teacher' was the front-page headline of the *Daily Mail*. Of course, this was a tragedy. The death of any 18-year-old is a tragedy. But what I found also tragic was that we appear to have learnt nothing, even though this particular drug has been widely used for the last 10 years. The way that this case was reported revealed the confusion and hypocrisy that strangles at birth any sensible debate about drugs. Julia Dawes should not have died. She was good-looking; her parents went to church; she had everything going for her. She was

not a member of the under-class. She did not live on a sink estate. What is more, she was a fitness instructor who cared about her body. How then did she come to take this drug? Predictably, someone has to pay, and four people have been arrested on charges of supplying her with it.

The reports reminded us too of another 'innocent', Leah Betts. She shouldn't have died either and her face became the face of a campaign to persuade other youngsters not to take Ecstasy. Leah Betts became what the writer Andrew O'Hagan called 'the patron saint of ignorance'. That may offend some people, yet the campaign waged in her name has been, however you want to measure it, a failure. It has not deterred people her age from taking Ecstasy because in their experience you don't die and their experience is that a hell of a lot of people take it every weekend and live to tell the tale. If clubbers are using less Ecstasy than they were a few years ago, it is not because they

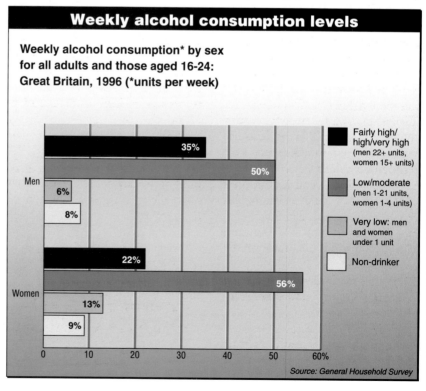

Weekly alcohol consumption levels

Weekly alcohol consumption* by sex for all adults and those aged 16-24: Great Britain, 1996 (*units per week)

Men
- 35%
- 50%
- 6%
- 8%

Women
- 22%
- 56%
- 13%
- 9%

0 — 10 — 20 — 30 — 40 — 50 — 60%

- Fairly high/high/very high (men 22+ units, women 15+ units)
- Low/moderate (men 1-21 units, women 1-4 units)
- Very low: men and women under 1 unit
- Non-drinker

Source: General Household Survey

have been frightened off but because the quality of the drug has deteriorated.

'We find it hard to believe that Julia would have been involved with drugs in any way' said a friend of the family. We have been down this path before and it leads only to dead ends. Richard Benson wrote in 1996 in *The Face*, a magazine that does not find it hard to believe that nice girls like Leah and Julia may use drugs 'We walk now in a veiled land…'. The veil he was referring to was the veil that exists between a world in which drugs are commonplace, part of a youth culture, and a world which denies or demonises their use.

The death of Leah Betts proved how near and yet how far these worlds are from one another. As Benson wrote 'On the night she took Ecstasy… she was sitting in her Mum's and Dad's living room having a birthday party while they sat in the kitchen. When the veil was lifted, it was found that the veiled and unveiled worlds were not merely close to one another. They were the same.' Six teenagers have died after taking Ecstasy in the past 10 years; 55 after drinking too much alcohol. But could you tell which was the bigger danger, from reading newspapers? The world regards them differently.

The TV star Caroline Aherne admitted, after leaving a private clinic, that she was an alcoholic. Her treatment cost her £17,000, but she said it saved her life. Aherne's case was reported sympathetically. We like Mrs Merton and know she has had a hard time lately. Her 'confession' meant that she joined the expanding cast list of celebrity alcoholics. A few days earlier Kevin Kennedy, who plays Curly Watts in *Coronation Street*, had held a press conference at which he detailed his drink problem. He was promoted to face up to his addiction after Kevin Lloyd, Tosh in *The Bill*, drank himself to death in May. Three days before Lloyd died he had told a friend: 'I can't stop drinking now. I know it's killing me.'

Many lesser-known boozers drink themselves to death. They are the real alcoholics anonymous. We don't know where they are. We only

know that most of them certainly cannot afford to spend time recovering in private clinics. Our image of alcoholism is muddled to say the least, veering as it does between the bruised and battered winos we see gathered on park benches, and glamorous stars such as Liz Taylor and the model Paula Hamilton who bravely battle in public to stay clean and sober.

Ordinary alcoholism and the misery it causes is not something we pay much attention to. Perhaps it is too close to home. After all, alcohol is everywhere, and within our everyday experience. This is not some weird killer drug. It is our sanctified social lubricant. It is simply what we do, and just because some poor sods do it too much, doesn't mean that the rest of us shouldn't do it at all.

Politicians do not say much about alcohol. How can they? Huge amounts of revenue are raised in form of tax on drink. Anyway, alcohol is central to political culture. The bars of the House of Commons are full of those who, like many of us, drink to relax, drink because there is nothing better to do, drink in order to feel part of whatever it is that is going on. Edwina Currie once told me that when she first entered the House she was surprised to find that you spent most of the day not really drunk but not really sober either. So she stopped drinking.

One survey found that some 12-year-olds were drinking as much as 15 whiskies in a session

---

Yet the moral panic about drugs and the youth population, and the Government's refusal to talk sensibly about drugs policy, mean that we are not confronting what is really dangerous for our kids. Smoking, more than any other drug, kills, but smoking does not cause antisocial behaviour. Those who smoke know the risks they are taking. They are unlikely, because of their nasty habit, to cause death and destruction to anyone other than themselves. Drinking, on the other hand, has massive repercussions for the whole of society, as Dr Abraham of the Medical Council on Alcoholism has said: 'Alcohol diseases are hidden because alcohol is a legal drug. The social consequences (i.e. actions) of tobacco are minimal. In alcohol they're massive – crime, violence, accidents, divorce, family feuds.'

Addiction to alcohol wreaks havoc. Drunk drivers kill people; drunks start fights. The lagered-up lads of the market towns who start mini-riots every Saturday night would be less inclined to do so without alcohol. Much domestic violence and child abuse can be linked to the consumption of alcohol. Families are torn apart by this drug. Many of those we see sleeping in our streets have alcohol-related problems. All this happens far away from the Betty Ford clinic and the psycho-babble of the reformed celebrity drinker. It is horribly commonplace.

Deaths from alcohol-related diseases have increased by more than a third in the last ten years. Between 1984 and 1994 the number of deaths from alcoholic liver disease doubled in those aged between 15 and 44. All trends show that young people, especially young women, are drinking more and are beginning to drink earlier. Last year the Health Authority published figures that showed that three-quarters of all 11-year-olds had tried alcohol. One survey found that some 12-year-olds were drinking as much as 15 whiskies in a session.

Perhaps because alcohol is everywhere and freely available as part of mainstream culture, we would prefer to worry about other intoxicants that we believe may harm our children. Yet even a cursory glance at the statistics shows that we may be getting things out of proportion. Figures vary, but it is estimated that over 5,000 deaths a year in England and Wales are directly related to alcohol. Compare this with deaths from other drugs. Although the figures are rising, in the whole of the United Kingdom in 1995, the total deaths from heroin were 319. In the same year, the number of deaths directly attributable to Ecstasy were six. Even this week, with the predictable scaremongering that followed Julia Dawes's death, experts estimated that though 1.5 million young people are taking Ecstasy every week, the death toll this year is unlikely to be more than 20.

Statistics may be meaningless when faced with the loss of a vibrant child, but nonetheless we cannot afford to become so mired in hypocrisy that we exaggerate the risks of illegal drugs and gloss over the risks of the legal ones. We know from all the evidence that prohibition does not work. While the Government pursues variants of the Just Say No campaign, drug agencies have moved on to a Just Say Know approach, trying to give drug users information about the substances they are taking. If we are going to drink, then we need not only to inform ourselves of the risks, but also to be clearer about the signs of addiction. We need to recognise when social drinking spills over into something more problematic.

Those who drink know that alcohol can be immensely pleasurable – one of life's joys. Those who take drugs know the same thing. Sometimes, though, it gets ugly. Indeed, rave culture grew up partly as a reaction to the aggression and out-of-control laddishness of drink culture. I find it astonishing that the Government, headed by people in their early forties, can continue to perpetuate the myth of two separate cultures even when faced with the drug use of their own children. Those children may know that the drugs their parents consume legally may be ultimately more life-threatening and socially devastating than the illegal ones that they prefer, but can we honestly say that the rest of us are as well informed?

Alcohol problems and work statistics

Information from Alcohol Concern

Money
- Total expenditure on alcohol, UK 1995 £26,763 million
- Government revenue from alcohol, UK 1995 £9,745.9 million
- Social costs of alcohol misuse, 1990 £2,461.42 million
- Annual cost of alcohol-related sickness absence £964.37 million

Consumption
- Consumption of alcohol per head, UK 1960 4.4 litres
- Consumption of alcohol per head, UK 1995 7.2 litres

Risk drinking
- 27% of men in Great Britain drink more than the medically recommended level of 21 units a week.
- 13% of women in Great Britain drink more than the medically recommended level of 14 units a week.
- 6% of men in Great Britain drink more than 50 units a week.
- 2% of women drink more than 35 units a week.

Consequences
- Over 2/3 (70%) of employers say alcohol misuse is a problem in their organisation, a slight fall from a similar survey in 1992.
- Up to 25% of accidents at work involve intoxicated workers.
- 8 to 14 million days are lost each year as a result of alcohol-related problems.
- In a 1989 survey by OPCS, 11% of working men and 6% of working women admitted that they had had a drink during working hours in the seven days before interview.
- In the same survey, 4% of male respondents and 2% of female respondents admitted to taking time off work because of a hangover at least once in the previous year.
- And 7% of men and 3% of women admitted that their work had been below par because of drinking in the last year.
- One study found that men drinking over 21 units a week take twice as much sick leave, measured both in total episodes (spells) and total duration (days) as men drinking less than 21 units.

Employment
- In Great Britain in 1995, employment in the brewing and related industries was 1,065,000.

Social costs of alcohol

Costs to society

- NHS responses to alcohol-related health problems cost around £150 million per year.
- Alcohol-related crime costs the government an estimated £50 million per year.
- Alcohol misuse costs industry an estimated £2 billion per year.

Health

- One in four male hospital admissions is related in some way to alcohol.
- Death from liver disease is ten times more common in heavy drinkers than in non-drinkers.
- While drinking within the recommended limits (21 units a week for men, 14 units a week for women) may protect middle-aged men against heart disease, drinking above the limits is probably the commonest cause of high blood pressure, and it increases the risk of stroke and other forms of heart disease.
- About 3% of all cancers may be attributable to alcohol.

Deaths

- Up to 28,000 deaths a year are alcohol-related. As well as over 3,000 cases with alcohol specified on the death certificate, this figure includes suicides and accidents, and allows for the diseases to which alcohol contributes – some cancers, strokes etc.
- A substantial proportion of accidents and violence – the major causes of death in young men – are alcohol-related.
- Alcohol is involved in about 15% of traffic deaths, 26% of drownings and 39% of deaths in fires.

Drinking and driving

- The continued campaign against drink-driving has reduced deaths on the roads caused by drinking, to 510 in 1994 (from over 1,650 in 1979) – but still one in seven of all road deaths.

- Only 14% of people breath tested failed in 1993, the lowest proportion yet recorded, and a significant drop from the 42% recorded in 1984.

Mental health

- Over 4,500 men and women were admitted to mental hospitals with alcohol-related problems in 1986 (the last year for which figures are available).
- About 65% of suicide attempts are linked with excessive drinking.

Families

- Alcohol has been noted as a factor in 20% to 40% of child abuse cases, sometimes more.
- Alcohol is involved in 40% of domestic violence incidents.
- Separated and divorced men drink more heavily than married or single men, with 39% drinking over the recommended levels. While this could mean that marriage breakdown leads to increased drinking, it is also likely that many of these men were heavy drinkers before the breakdown.

Crime

- A recent survey of probation officers found that nearly 30% of their clients, and 58% of remand and sentenced prisoners, have severe problems with alcohol.
- Research shows that offenders are intoxicated in 30% of sexual offences, 33% of burglaries, 50% of crime in the street, 85% of crime in pubs or clubs.
- Either offender or victim have been drinking in 65% of murders and 75% of stabbings.
- Studies in urban areas have shown that almost half of incidents of disorderly behaviour occur shortly after the pubs close, especially on Friday and Saturday nights, and often involve young men.
- 59,900 people were found guilty or cautioned for drunkenness in 1993; the peak age for drunkenness offences is 19-20 years.

Workplace

- 75% of employers say alcohol misuse is a problem in their organisation.
- Up to 25% of accidents at work involve intoxicated workers.
- 8-14 million days are lost each year as a result of alcohol-related problems.
- 7% of men and 3% of women admitted that their work had been below par because of drinking in the last year.

© Alcohol Concern

What too much drink does to you

Revealed

Most people have probably indulged themselves a little too much on their summer holiday – particularly when it came to the odd drink. And it's all too easy to continue drinking at the same rate when you're back home. Figures show that 14pc of women drink 20 glasses of wine – or 20 units of alcohol – a week, while a similar number of men drink 16 pints of lager or spirit shots (32 units) a week. Both are double the safe alcohol levels of ten units a week for women and 16 for men. Becky Morris looks at the effects on the body if those levels are sustained over a month.

Women

Mental health

One in six women suffers from depression in their lifetime, and alcohol can exacerbate this. 'Alcohol is a stimulant in the short term but a depressant in the long term,' says Dr Sarah Jarvis of Alcohol Concern. If you drink too much for a month, it will leave you feeling more depressed. And if you use alcohol to escape existing depression, you will only make it worse, she warns.

Weight

Alcohol causes weight gain because it is rich in calories. Dry white wine has 85 calories a glass, champagne 95 and sweet white wine 120. So a 20-glass-a-week habit could mean an extra 1,700 calories a week – or 7,300 a month.

Every 3,500 extra calories cause a 1lb weight gain, so a 20-glass-a-week drinker could gain 2lb in a month on dry white wine, or nearly 3lb on sweet white wine.

'Alcohol can also disrupt your eating patterns because it causes blood sugar to drop,' says Lyndel Costain of the British Dietetic Association. 'This can cause people to get the 'munchies' after an evening's drinking or on the morning after, leading you to eat unhealthy things such as kebabs or a fried breakfast.'

Skin

Women's skin is thinner than men's, so the effects of drinking on the complexion are more marked. Alcohol also dilates blood capillaries which can cause the face to flush while drinking.

'After a month of drinking at this kind of level, your general ill-health will almost certainly show in your skin, in terms of lack of condition, dryness, spots and other blemishes,' says Dr Jarvis.

Pancreas

Inflammation of the pancreas, known as pancreatitis, can occur in as little as a month, depending on your genetic make-up. Women's pancreas are 50pc more vulnerable to alcohol damage than men's.

Symptoms include severe pain in the upper abdomen, with nausea and vomiting. Chronic pancreatitis can cause permanent damage to the pancreas and result in it having to be surgically removed.

Kidneys

Alcohol acts as a diuretic – encouraging fluid to leave the body in the form of urine – so prolonged heavy drinking can cause kidney problems,

or even renal failure. 'Like the liver, other major organs such as the kidneys, the pancreas and the brain are more at risk from alcohol damage in women, and damage can take place in as little as two years in women,' says alcohol specialist Dr Michael Glynn of the Royal London Hospital.

Liver

Women's livers are 50pc more vulnerable to alcohol than men's, says Dr Glynn.

The earliest sign of trouble is the accumulation of fat globules in the liver – something found in nearly all moderate to heavy drinkers.

The next stage of damage is hepatitis (inflammation of the liver). 'It very much depends on one's genetic propensity, but for some people it is possible to develop hepatitis in as little as a month of drinking too much,' says Dr Glynn.

'There may be no symptoms at all, or just a feeling of discomfort and nausea. The best way to find out how your liver is doing is to ask your GP for a liver-function test.'

If drinking persists on a damaged liver, scarring results, and this can lead to cirrhosis. 'Women are much more prone to this than men – the usual time scale is five years of drinking before cirrhosis develops, but in some women it can be as little as two years,' says Dr Glynn.

Men

Blood pressure

Men are much more prone to hypertension than women, and can expect an increase in blood pressure after a month's over-indulgence. After many years of heavy drinking, this could lead to a stroke – damage to the brain caused by an interruption of its blood supply. Men are more at risk from strokes than women because they lack the protective effect of the hormone oestrogen.

Mental health

Alcohol depresses the central nervous system which is why, in the short term, it reduces inhibitions and tension. But a month's drinking at this rate will interfere with the balance of chemicals in the brain, lowering its production of serotonin, which regulates mood. This leads to mild symptoms of depression, including insomnia. Feelings of sluggishness, anxiety and loss of concentration at work are also likely.

Weight

Testosterone in men makes weight gain more common around the stomach and abdomen, resulting in a beer belly. Ordinary beer contains about 170 calories a pint, while strong lager has as much as 400 calories a pint. For every 3,500 calories you consume over the calorie intake required, you will gain 1lb. This means that a 16-pint-a-week habit of ordinary strength lager could lead to almost 1lb a week in weight gain.

This can have serious health implications because the fat in a beer belly is more easily broken down into the blood stream than fat on the hips. 'Apple-shaped people have been found to have a greater chance of developing diabetes and high blood pressure than pear-shaped people, who gain weight around their hips and thighs,' says Lyndel Costain of the British Dietetic Association.

Heart

Men are more prone to coronary heart disease than women, although the gap is closing. In the long term, a high alcohol intake increases the likelihood of damage to the heart. A regular, moderate intake of alcohol – two to three units a day – has been found to protect against strokes and heart disease, but this benefit is lost when drinking more heavily.

Liver

After a month, men will notice that they are able to drink more than they previously could without feeling drunk. This tolerance develops because the liver learns to break down alcohol at a faster rate, so more drinks are needed to achieve the same alcohol level in the blood. This activity upsets the liver's enzyme balance causing it to swell with fatty globules, thus increasing weight gain. As alcohol is broken down, it produces a toxic chemical called acetaldehyde, which attacks the liver.

Digestive system

Gastritis, the inflammation of the stomach lining, is a common result of binge drinking, and is more prevalent among men, particularly in the 18 to 24-year-old age group. This causes severe nausea, vomiting and abdominal discomfort and can become a permanent problem. The irritant action of alcohol – even over just one month – can create peptic ulcers. These are more common in men, and are thought to be linked to their higher stress levels.

Skin

Drinking like this over a month could give you greasy, even blemished skin. Alcohol also dries the scalp, giving you severe dandruff. It can also lead to hair loss.

Puffy, bloated faces are also a sign of over-indulgence. This is because alcohol acts as a diuretic, forcing water to leave the body in the form of urine. This stresses the kidneys, causing imbalances in the body's salts, which in turn upset the balance of fluid in the cells – particularly in the face.

Effects on your fertility

Women

A recent study has discovered that even low consumption of alcohol – ten glasses of wine a week – can make it harder for a woman to conceive.

The research found that women who drink five units a week are twice as likely to conceive as women drinking ten or more.

Alcohol may disrupt the ability of a fertilised egg to implant in the womb.

Just a few months of heavy drinking can also cause heavy, less regular periods and lower the chances of ovulation, making conception more difficult.

Men

Drinking to excess in the long term depresses the sperm count.

'It's a secondary effect of liver disorder; moderation is crucial if you want to conceive easily and quickly,' says Professor Ian Craft of the London Fertility Centre.

In persistent heavy drinkers, 'feminisation' of the body occurs – breasts develop and the testicles shrivel as the liver produces globulin, which destroys sex hormones.

'Twenty years' hard drinking is needed to achieve this,' says Professor Craft.

© *The Daily Mail*
September, 1998

20 questions on sensible drinking

Information from The Portman Group

1. 'Sensible drinking' – isn't that a contradiction in terms?

Don't be misled by the bad image alcohol sometimes attracts. Like air travel, it only hits the headlines when something goes wrong. Alcohol misuse is a problem for a minority. The majority of those who drink do so responsibly.

2. Isn't it a bit dreary though?

Thanks to research studies, we now know much more about how to drink in a way that is compatible with a healthy lifestyle. We also know more about the health and other risks we run if we ignore that information. So 'sensible drinking' is a way of enjoying the pleasure and the benefits, but avoiding the hazards and the harm.

3. Is it true the Government has put up my weekly alcohol allowance?

No! The latest guidelines abolish weekly limits altogether. Instead, they give us daily benchmarks.

4. So what's a daily benchmark?

It's the amount of alcohol that the Government's Sensible Drinking guidelines say that most people can drink in a day without putting your health at risk. But it's a guide, not a target.

5. So I could still take it easy during the week and use up my 'allowance' on Saturday night?

No again. Since the old guidelines (which used to give weekly limits), new research has shown how harmful 'binge drinking' can be. There's a world of difference between drinking, say, a pint of beer or a glass of wine every day, and going without during the week just to get plastered on 7 pints or a whole bottle of wine on Saturday night. It's not just the amount, it's how you spread it out that counts.

6. So how much is OK to drink each day?

That depends on whether you're male or female. Most men are OK for 3 to 4 units a day, most women for 2 to 3. But if men consistently drink 4 or more units a day, the health risks start to accumulate. The same goes for women who consistently drink 3 or more units a day.

7. Units? What on earth are units?

Units are a way of measuring how much alcohol you're drinking. A unit is 8 grams of pure alcohol, if you want to be scientific about it. But the amount of alcohol in any given type of drink will obviously depend on how big the glass, can or bottle is, and how strong the drink is.

8. I'm no Einstein. How can I keep track of my units without being a whiz-kid at maths?

Luckily, most drinks come in fairly standard sizes and strengths. So it's quite easy to keep an accurate enough tally – if you're drinking out, that is. If you're having spirits or wine at home, though, you'll need to be more alert, as you can bet you'll be helping yourself to larger servings than the pub or restaurant would give you! The examples in The Portman Group's leaflet 'It all adds up' give

the most workable unit ranges, to the nearest half-unit, for the most common drinks in the most common servings. You could use that as a ready reckoner.

9. Can you give me some 'rule of thumb' example?

Sure: half a pint of ordinary strength beer is 1 unit. A single pub measure of spirits is also 1 unit. A small glass of 11% ABV wine is 1.5 units.

10. How would I work all this out for myself?

If you want to do the arithmetic accurately yourself, the formula is to multiply the amount of liquid (volume), measured in mls, by the alcoholic strength, measured in percentage ABV. Then you divide the total by 1000 to get the number of units. Some drinks have unit information on the label, to save you the trouble.

11. Surely different people can tolerate different amounts of alcohol?

Of course there are individual differences. Some people shouldn't drink at all. Children under 16 should not assume these guidelines apply to them either, as their bodies have not yet matured enough to deal with alcohol in the same way as adults. But the scientific research on which the guidelines are based does enable advice to be given both to men in general and women in general.

12. Are there any other exceptions to the rule?

People involved in certain activities where safety and control are paramount are advised not to drink at all. Driving is an obvious one. Before swimming or other active physical sports is another no-go area for drinking. And you shouldn't drink if you're about to operate machinery, go up ladders or do any kind of work which requires you to have your wits fully about you. Taking certain medications is also incompatible with drinking alcohol.

13. Why shouldn't women drink as much as men?

A woman drinking the same amount as a man of exactly the same size will get intoxicated faster because she has a lower proportion of water in her body weight. This leads to a higher concentration of alcohol in the body tissue. Women's average weight is lower than men's in any case. And just for good measure, the scientists also think that women's bodies break alcohol down more slowly than men's, so alcoholic drink has a longer-lasting effect.

14. Is it OK to drink in pregnancy?

If you're pregnant – or planning to be – then you've got to be sensible for two. The guidelines say that no more than 1 or 2 units once or twice a week should be the benchmark for you. Drunkenness should also be avoided, which should be easy enough if you're sticking to those guidelines.

15. I thought drinking red wine every day was supposed to be good for your heart. There must be some good news in here somewhere . . . ?

Well, the reference to red wine is a bit of a red herring. The good news is that it's any kind of alcohol, not just wine, that can have a significant protective effect on your heart. The bad news for all you strapping young twenty- or thirty-somethings out there is that the health benefit only kicks in for men over 40 and for women after the menopause.

16. Does that mean we can drink more as we get older?

Afraid not. It's important to remember that the maximum health advantage for the heart for men over 40 and women past the menopause comes from drinking between 1 and 2 units a day. Drinking more doesn't increase the benefit.

17. Why should I believe anything the Government advises?

The Government didn't just pluck the figures out of the air. The advice in the guidelines was drawn up after considering 89 written submissions, 43 of which came from scientific, academic or medical sources; 21 from the health promotion field and service providers, 9 from the drinks industry and 16 others.

18. It's all so complicated. Wouldn't it just be easier – and more honest – to get everyone to drink less?

Some people believe that if less alcohol were consumed by the population as a whole, there would be fewer alcohol-related problems. But this doesn't necessarily follow. Take the example of deaths caused by drink-driving in the UK. The numbers have dropped dramatically without the overall level of alcohol consumption going down. This has been achieved because people have responded positively to well-communicated messages about their behaviour. By the same token, people are more likely to continue drinking sensibly, or begin to drink sensibly, if they are informed by a general public health message which they can interpret in relation to their own personal behaviour and choices. They don't want to feel punished or guilty or nagged because of other people's over-indulgence, when they are doing no harm to their own health.

19. Are you seriously telling me that the drinks industry supports sensible drinking? What's in it for them?

You could put that the other way round: what's in it for the drinks industry if it does nothing about the way a minority of people misuse its products? The major alcoholic drinks companies set up The Portman Group in 1989 because they were genuinely committed to promoting sensible drinking and helping to prevent alcohol abuse. Our policies and work are carried out irrespective of the commercial consequences to the industry.

20. But they wouldn't fund The Portman Group if you weren't helping the industry, would they?

Exactly. And we believe that promoting sensible drinking, as well as being a worthwhile activity in its own right, is also in the long-term interests of the industry. Call it enlightened self-interest. If consumers and the industry can both benefit from the same approach, perhaps being sensible is not such a dreary idea after all. Being responsible and getting pleasure are not mutually exclusive activities. Sensible drinking is one way to do both.

• The above information is from The Portman Group. See page 41 for address details.

© The Portman Group
March, 1998

Too much drink?

Information from the Health Education Authority (HEA)

Think

A campaign to raise awareness of the harm caused by drunkenness is launched today as new research reveals that more than 9 million men and 6.2 million women have been drunk over the last year. Almost a million men get drunk at least once a week compared to less than 190,000 women.

The research has been released to mark the start of *Too Much Drink? Think*, a Health Education Authority (HEA) campaign to show that many alcohol-related problems are caused by one-off periods of heavy drinking. These include accidents and injuries, blackouts and memory loss, alcohol poisoning, sickness and hangovers, crime and violence, and doing something you later regret, including having unprotected sex.

Sixteen to 24-year-olds are the most likely to binge drink, do something they regret, have a row or feel aggressive after drinking, with more than three-quarters of this age group – equivalent to more than 4.5 million people – admitting to getting drunk.

But the research also found risky drinking behaviour among all adult drinkers, with almost six out of ten men saying they had drunk the equivalent of four pints or more in one session – equivalent to 8 or more units – over the past year. More than a third of women had drunk the equivalent of 3 pints (6 units) or more in one session.

The HEA is promoting a range of steps people can take to cut down and survive the party season. If people do overdo it, the best advice is not to drink any alcohol for 48 hours to give the body time to recover.

For the campaign, the HEA has produced a series of posters focusing on getting home safely, the workplace, violence and social embarrassment. It has also produced a range of postcards – 'puke', 'snot', 'prat', 'scrap' – targeting underage drinkers. These will have nation-wide cinema distribution to coincide with release of the Spice Girls movie.

The campaign has the backing of a range of health, medical and industry groups, and shows that drunkenness is risky not just for individuals, but for families, workplaces and communities.

Campaign Manager, Andy Seale, said: 'Getting drunk is more than a health risk. It can damage your career, your studies, relationships, reputation and self-respect.

'Alcohol is a central part of our social life – our research shows three-quarters of the adult population have been to a pub or club and had a drink in the past year. But while it often causes no problems, drinking too much or at the wrong time is always risky.'

Key findings from the research, based on interviews with more than 1,600 adults, include:

- One in five men who drink admitted to having an argument after drinking during the past year. More than a third had witnessed a fight between people who had been drinking.
- Almost a third of men and more than a quarter of women who drink said they had started drinking with the intention of getting drunk in the past year.

- More than half of men and more than two-thirds of women said they would or might leave a party because people were getting drunk.
- More than a third of men and 44 per cent of women said they would feel 'on edge' if, when out with friends, they encountered a group of people they didn't know who were drunk.

Among 16-24-year-olds the research found:

- 81 per cent of male drinkers had drunk the equivalent of four or more pints in a session – more than half of these said they did so at least once a week. Sixty per cent of young women had drunk the equivalent of three or more pints in a session – more than a quarter did so at least once a week
- 31 per cent of men who drink said they felt more aggressive after drinking
- 42 per cent of men and a quarter of women drinkers said they had argued after drinking
- almost seven out of ten men and women (68 per cent) in this age group said they had witnessed a fight after people had been drinking
- one in ten male drinkers admitted injuring themselves because of an accident after drinking

When asked what they meant by 'drunk', more than half of all men and women said it meant 'not in control'. Other popular responses were feeling 'light-headed' and 'slurred speech'. However, just 29 per cent thought that getting drunk was 'part of the English way of life'.

Andy Seale added: 'Getting drunk needn't be an inevitable part of having a good time. We hope this campaign will help to encourage greater respect for alcohol.'

Alcohol summary facts

Information from the Health Education Authority (HEA)

Young people (under 17)

A Health Education Authority (HEA) survey of 11-16-year-olds in 1995 found that 74% of 11-year-olds, and virtually all (96%) 15-year-olds had tasted an alcoholic drink. Findings from an HEA survey in 1989 suggest that:

- about 900,000 children (aged 11-15) in England have had an alcoholic drink in the 'last week'.
- in an average week in England, 35,000 children under the age of 16 consume alcohol in excess of the adult sensible weekly limits (at the time of the 1989 HEA survey this was 21 units per week for males, 14 units per week for females).
- 1 in 10 (11-15-year-olds) drink regularly with their parents.
- an estimated 130,000 children under the age of 16 drink alcohol in pubs in an average week in England.

Adults(16 and over)

- 93% of men and 86% of women aged 16 and over claim to drink alcohol in Great Britain.
- In 1994, 27% of men and 13% of women were drinking above the then recommended sensible limits (21 units per week for men and 14 units for women): this is the equivalent of around 9 million adults aged 18+ in England.

The HEA's Health Education Monitoring Survey among adults (aged 16-74) in 1995 found that:

- 80% claimed to be aware of the term 'units of alcohol'. Of these, only between a quarter and a third were able to give the correct numbers of units in different drink measures.
- Of those who had heard of units of alcohol, only 20% of men and 17% of women could state correctly the number of units recommended at that time as the sensible level for men (21 units); only 14% of men and 21% of women could give the recommended levels for women (14 units).

Alcohol and health

Current recommended daily benchmarks are up to between 3-4 units per day for men, and up to between 2-3 units per day for women. These benchmarks apply whether someone drinks every day, once or twice a week, or occasionally.

Regularly drinking 4 units a day (men) and 3 units a day (women) poses a progressive risk to health.

Estimates of alcohol-related deaths in England and Wales have ranged from 5,000 to 40,000 per year.

It has been estimated that 3% of all cancers might be attributable to alcohol.

It is estimated that 510 people died in drink-drive accidents in Great Britain in 1994. Another 14,590 people were injured in such accidents.

The British Crime Survey showed that in 44% of incidents of violence, the victim said the offender was drunk.

Men over 40 and women who have been through the menopause may benefit from a significant reduction in risk of coronary heart disease if they drink between 1 and 2 units a day.

Moderate drinking also protects against ischaemic stroke and may inhibit cholesterol-type gallstones, but increases risk of haemorrhagic stroke.

The economic cost of alcohol

The cost to industry in terms of sickness absence due to alcohol was estimated to be about £1059 million in 1992.

Between 8.8 and 14.8 million working days are lost to industry each year through alcohol-related illness.

It has been estimated that alcohol misuse costs society £2.7 billion per year (at 1992 prices).

Alcohol industry: price and sales

- The UK alcoholic drinks market was worth £25.8 billion at retail prices in 1994.
- In 1994, the UK industry spent £114.8 million on the advertising of alcoholic beverages.
- England and Wales has one public house for every 554 adults aged 16 and over.
- In 1994, UK consumer expenditure on alcohol was 4.3% of total expenditure.

© Health Education Authority (HEA), 1998

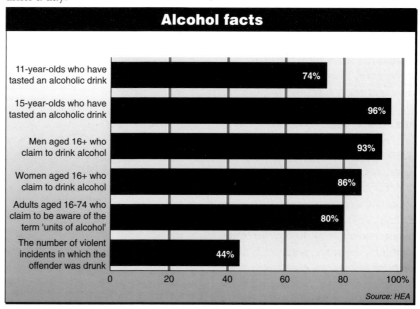

Alcohol facts

11-year-olds who have tasted an alcoholic drink	74%
15-year-olds who have tasted an alcoholic drink	96%
Men aged 16+ who claim to drink alcohol	93%
Women aged 16+ who claim to drink alcohol	86%
Adults aged 16-74 who claim to be aware of the term 'units of alcohol'	80%
The number of violent incidents in which the offender was drunk	44%

Source: HEA

Too much teen spirit

Teenagers drink too much. But how to curb them, in a society awash with alcohol?

By Jerome Burne

There is no evidence that my 16-year-old son is keen on house-work, so when he declared that he had spent an hour cleaning the bathroom I said I was impressed.

'I haven't been polishing the taps or anything like that,' he explained. 'I've been wiping Martin's vomit off the walls. It was disgusting. I'm not having him to a party again.'

Ben had had the house to himself and some friends for the night and the bathroom had been one of the casualties. This rite of passage for both of us could be interpreted in several ways. A valuable learning experience for Ben, seeing the effects of binge drinking all too close up, possibly a warning to his younger brother Jack, and to us as irresponsible parents, letting children run wild.

The dilemmas around how best to handle children and drink have been brought into sharp focus by the report that teenage alcohol consumption has increased by 40 per cent in the last five years. The likes of Ben and Jack are apparently drinking three more units a week than their predecessors were in 1993, and a third of them drink at home without the parents knowing. What's needed, say the experts, is more education. But, as I discovered, this can be hard to come by.

I called the NUS, who declared that they were certainly on the case as far as student drinking was concerned. Why, only last year they had run a campaign that involved dishing out glasses and posters to all universities with the logo 2F3M4. This was to remind students that the sensible daily amount for females was two units and for males, three to four. Wasn't it true, I asked, that the best way to reduce consumption was to raise prices? And didn't the NUS run subsidised bars? 'Er, yes,' admitted a slightly flustered spokesperson. 'But the prices are not so much lower that anyone would be encouraged to go bananas.'

So was there any evidence that the posters and mugs were having any effect? 'We don't keep any information like that,' I was told. 'We just act as a conduit. The people you need to talk to are Drinkline. They run a help line and do all the research.' But a call to Drinkline was no more enlightening. 'I'm afraid we are about to close,' said another harassed-sounding spokesperson. 'Drinkline is out to tender.'

> **'There are cut-price drinks for students somewhere in town every night, but I've never seen any material about sensible drinking'**

So I turned to see what was being done in America, where concern and consumption rates are similar. For instance, a recent study by the Harvard School of Public Health showed that 70 per cent of students at some college campuses 'binge drink' – defined as having five drinks in a row for males, and four for females. This compares with *The Lancet*'s 1996 survey which found excessive and binge drinking among 50 per cent of students. Interestingly, among non-white UK students only 3 per cent drank heavily. A study by the marvellously named American organisation Madd (Mothers Against Drunk Driving) estimated that half of schoolchildren drink.

There's no shortage of research to suggest we should be alarmed by this torrent of booze disappearing down teenage throats. Take the physical effects. While processing alcohol – at the rate of one hour per drink for a 160-lb adult male – the liver can't do its normal job of releasing stored energy. So you get tired. Your liver is threatened because there is more iron in your blood, and you won't be building bone and muscle at the rate you should. What's more, drinking regularly means you will be extracting fewer vitamins from your meals, at a time when you're not only growing, but are probably eating badly anyway.

'Boring,' retort the 16-year-olds clutching cans of lager outside a football ground, who rightly believe in their own immortality. What may make more of an impression is the finding that alcohol causes an increase in oestrogen levels in men and testosterone levels in females. Even in these politely correct times, becoming more of a girl if you are a boy, and vice versa, are generally viewed with alarm.

But research findings have an uncomfortable way of cutting both ways. In several American reports the following facts are cited as damning evidence against alcohol: 'Adolescents who reported misusing alcohol were likely to engage in early sexual activity, multiple partners, and unprotected intercourse 6.1 to 23.0 times more than young people who did not misuse alcohol.' Such behaviour is, of course, terribly irresponsible, but I can't help feeling the statistic may not have the deterrent effect it is supposed to.

British calls for more education seem to fall on deaf ears. There is provision for education on alcohol in the national curriculum, but experts admit that implementation is patchy. My informal research confirmed it. Ben commented: 'We were told about drinking at school, but it was a long time ago and I can't remember what was said.' Sulla, a 20-year-old at Nottingham University, remarked: 'Sure we all get drunk.

There are cut-price drinks for students somewhere in town every night, but I've never seen any material about sensible drinking.'

The budgets of those concerned about teenage drinking are minuscule compared with the vast coffers of the alcohol industry. How can a few posters with silly logos compete with glossy ads that pretend drinking vodka is like having an LSD trip, or news stories about footballing heroes getting out of it?

In the US, with more money – the Office of Alcohol and Other Substances has a $20m grant – and a stronger puritan tradition, there is rather more direct action. Sadd (Students Against Destructive Decisions) has got 'young people at more than 16,000 schools fighting alcohol abuse and drink-driving'. One of their posters reads: 'If you are going to drink and drive, then be sure to kiss your mother goodbye.' In a recent announcement Osap (Office of Substance Abuse Prevention), which vets information packs that go out to schools, demanded: '… materials recommending a designated driver be rated unacceptable. They encourage heavy alcohol use by implying it is OK to drink to intoxication as long as you don't drive.' Some universities now have limits on the amount of alcohol that can be brought on to campus, enforced with $50 and $100 fines. The claim is that this cuts the number of binge drinkers in half.

Some American campaigners say that a price hike is the simplest and most effective way to reduce heavy drinking. But it turns out not to be so simple. A study two years ago concluded: 'the drinking practices of male college students are generally insensitive to the price of beer [but] under-age drinking and drinking by female students do respond significantly to price'. Interestingly, while males cut back on binge drinking when tough drink-driving laws are enforced, females do not.

Given that our society is awash with alcohol, we can hardly expect teenagers not to experiment, and the long-term effects are uncertain. Some campaigners claim that heavy drinking as a teenager predicts

problems as an adult, while *The Lancet* is more circumspect: 'It remains unclear whether university students' lifestyles are carried over into later life.' There undoubtedly can be health problems, but who is more likely to be affected?

For what it's worth, my own view is that teenagers have to learn to negotiate their relationship with alcohol just as they do with the opposite sex, shopping and work. Most will make it OK, but a few will run into problems. Whatever happens, though, by the time they really need it, they won't take much notice of your advice. The best you can do is keep a loving connection with them.

'If you are going to drink and drive, then be sure to kiss your mother goodbye'

The Portman Group, an alcohol research institution funded by the industry, produced a booklet for parents last year that advised being relaxed with your children over alcohol, being honest about the pleasures and the risks and letting them try small amounts at home. Ben agreed that he was all in favour

of parents telling kids about drink: 'For instance, does chardonnay or cabernet sauvignon go with lobster, and what are the vintage years?'

How to tell if something's wrong

If your child does have a problem with alcohol, he or she may not admit it. Here are some questions that, if answered honestly, can reveal whether help is needed:

- Do you feel uncomfortable when alcohol isn't available?
- Do you ever miss school, work, or social activities because of alcohol?
- Do you spend much time hung over?
- Do you drink more than usual when you're under pressure?
- Do you binge drink?
- Do you ever feel guilty about drinking?
- Do you resent it when people talk about your drinking?
- Have you ever been unable to remember parts of the evening before?

Organisations to contact: The Portman Group (0171 499 1010); Alcohol Concern (0171 928 7377); Drinkline Youth National helpline (0345 320202 – while it remains open).

© The Independent
June, 1998

Type of drinks

Percentage consuming different types of alcoholic drinks in the last 12 months: adults aged 16-24

Source: Health in England 1996, HMSO

Alcopops – no soft options

Research shows the amount of alcohol that young people consume is increasing, and the finger of blame points to alcopops. Tim Burke investigates the measures being taken to discourage under-age drinking and curb the growth of the alcopops market

Nearly 70 per cent of 15-year-olds and 50 per cent of 10-year-olds had a drink last week – and alcopops are in the frame as contributing to a 10 per cent rise over the past year. A survey of some 8,000 young people by the Schools Health Education Unit (SHEU) at Exeter University showed that by age 15 those boys who admit to drinking drank on average 10 units a week, the equivalent of five pints of beer. Girls were only one pint equivalent behind. The SHEU has been tracking alcohol consumption for 10 years in an annual survey conducted in some 1,000 schools.

The survey findings have added to the current controversy over alcopops by indicating that those who drink alcopops consume around 50 per cent more units of alcohol per week than those who do not. Around half of young drinkers consume alcopops, and the survey found a strong association between alcopop drinking and drinking beers, wines and spirits. Some 72 per cent of 15-year-old boy alcopop drinkers also drank beer or lager in the previous week and 36 per cent drank spirits. Only 18 per cent mentioned drinking low alcohol beer and fewer still shandy or low alcohol wine.

Advice for adults is to limit drinking of alcohol to 28 units per week for men and 21 for women. Doctors are reluctant to give precise figures for young people because of the large differences in bodyweight.

'It would also deflect from the real problem which is about under-age sales and the promotion of alcohol among young people,' said British Medical Association spokesman Dr Bill O'Neill. 'There ought to be advice on sensible drinking and the context in which children are allowed to drink. Rigid guidelines would not be helpful.'

The BMA has also warned that if measures are not taken there could be an 'epidemic' of liver disease in 20 years' time. Other pressure groups, including Christian youth groups, have called for strict measures to control alcopops. The Salvation Army's newspaper for children, *Kids Alive*, has been running a campaign called Spiked and recently delivered 1,000 letters of protest from young people to the Home Office. Hope UK has urged the government to take a holistic view on alcohol

---

Nearly 70 per cent of 15-year-olds and 50 per cent of 10-year-olds had a drink last week

---

education and make it a priority to support the voluntary youth service to establish attractive alcohol-free facilities within existing buildings.

'A major reason why alcopops are so popular is because they offer a quick route to obtaining the effects of alcohol and this is why Hope UK believes it is essential to face up to the whole issue and not simply focus on the products,' ran a statement from the group.

The government has responded to increasing concern with alcopops by introducing measures it hopes will curb their growth. The law in England and Wales is to be brought into line with Scotland, making it an offence for an adult to buy alcohol for a juvenile. There will also be tougher restrictions on cornershop off-licences which will see them lose their licences if found to be selling alcohol to young people.

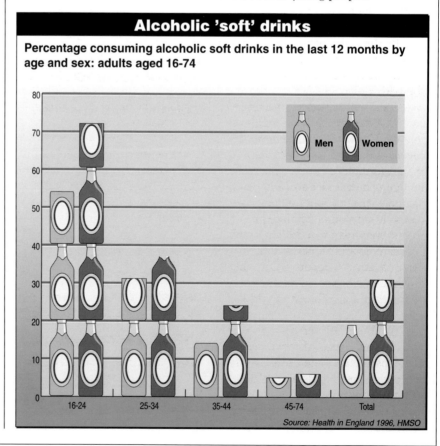

Alcoholic 'soft' drinks

Percentage consuming alcoholic soft drinks in the last 12 months by age and sex: adults aged 16-74

Source: Health in England 1996, HMSO

The government appears to have ruled out a ban on the products, although some supermarkets, including the Co-op and Iceland, have already withdrawn them from sale.

'While commercially this decision will hurt, we must act responsibly and reflect the views of our customers,' said Iceland chairman Malcolm Walker. 'There is definite evidence that these drinks are encouraging under-age drinking – this can't be tolerated.'

Tesco and Safeway decided not to withdraw the products but have said they will not carry in-store promotions, while Sainsbury's insists customers should have the choice although they will take measures to ensure checkout staff check the age of alcopop purchasers. The JD Wetherspoon pub chain is trying out a ban in selected pubs and may extend it to all branches.

Bass, which produces two-thirds of all alcopops, predictably rejected claims of targeting young people, and said opponents were demonising a product that was enjoyed responsibly by 'the vast majority' of consumers.

The drinks industry body, the Portman Group, has tightened up its marketing code and will prohibit packaging that has connotations of illicit drugs or sexual prowess or which uses imagery, colours or typography attractive to under-25s.

• *Young people and Alcohol: its use and abuse* is available, priced £17.00, from the Schools Health Education Unit, Renslade House, Bonhay Road, Exeter, Devon EX4 3AY

© *Young People Now*
September, 1997

11-year-olds get drinking habit with 'alcopops'

By David Fletcher, Health Correspondent

Alcopops are getting children as young as 11 into the habit of drinking alcohol, according to a report published today.

A survey of more than 3,300 children under 16 says that one in 10 of 11 and 12-year-old boys, and one in 13 girls of the same age, say they drink alcoholic soft drinks at least once a week.

By the time they reach 15 and 16, the girls overtake the boys, with nearly one in three girls saying that they drink alcopops at least once a week compared with one in four boys.

The report, by the publicly-funded Health Promotion Wales, shows that while alcohol use has increased across a range of products, including beer, cider and wine, it is alcopops that account for about half the consumption of youngsters.

It shows that in 1996, 65 per cent of boys and 54 per cent of girls aged 15 and 16 reported drinking alcohol on a regular weekly basis – an increase of 16 per cent on 10 years ago.

Of those, 30 per cent of girls and 24 per cent of boys drank alcopops at least once a week. Only four per cent of the girls drank alcohol other than alcopops.

The figures are based on answers by children in 48 schools in Wales for the Welsh Youth Health Survey which is carried out every two years. It shows that children are getting drunk more frequently.

In 1986, 38 per cent of boys and 24 per cent of girls said they had been drunk four or more times. By 1996 the figures were 53 per cent of boys and 43 per cent of girls.

Virginia Blakey, head of development at Health Promotion Wales, said that alcopops had gained a sizeable market among under-16s and were fuelling the problem of under-age drinking and producing serious health dangers.

She called on manufacturers to be aware that their products were widely consumed by under-16s and to change their marketing strategies to reduce the appeal of the drinks to children.

---

200 children were admitted to one Liverpool hospital last year with alcohol overdoses – a ten-fold increase since the 1980s

---

She added: 'It is important that their parents and other adults appreciate that alcopops, because they are more palatable to children than conventional alcoholic drinks, can help to establish behaviour likely to be very damaging to the health of children.'

The report is released in the same week as a Channel 4 programme which claims that hospitals are having to deal with a rising number of youngsters suffering from alcohol poisoning.

The programme, *Health Alert: Mine's an Alcopop*, to be transmitted on Thursday, will show doctors' concerns at the teenage trend.

It says that 200 children were admitted to one Liverpool hospital last year with alcohol overdoses – a tenfold increase since the 1980s.

• One in four children as young as 11 worries about being overweight, the Royal College of Nursing says in a report today. A MORI survey found 45 per cent of schoolgirls are anxious about being overweight compared with 21 per cent of boys.

It said children also worry increasingly about the appearance of their skin as they get older.

© *Telegraph Group Limited*
May, 1997

Alcopops 'not to blame for luring the young'

By David Fletcher, Health Correspondent

Alcopops are not to blame for the rise in drinking by children under the age of 16, says a Government study.

It said the fizzy alcoholic drinks are being drunk alongside beer, cider and lager but are not luring youngsters to alcohol when they would otherwise have stuck to soft drinks.

A survey by the Office for National Statistics published yesterday showed the amount of alcohol drunk by children aged 11-15 more than doubled in the past seven years and alcopops made up about one-sixth of the intake.

But the proportion of youngsters who drink alcohol has not changed, countering criticisms that alcopops are encouraging youngsters to drink. The number of youngsters who have never tried alcohol has remained virtually static at about 38 per cent.

The survey found that alcopops were likely to be more popular among children looking for drinks that masked the taste of alcohol.

Only one per cent of children said they drank only alcopops and there was no evidence to support claims that alcopops were particularly attractive to young drinkers.

Overall, beer, lager and cider accounted for 57 per cent of the alcohol drunk, alcopops for 17 per cent, spirits 14 per cent, wine eight per cent, fortified wine two per cent and shandy two per cent. Alcopop makers have been accused of deliberately targeting youngsters since launching the drinks in 1995.

Eileen Goddard, author of the report, said youngsters were drinking alcopops with other drinks, not to replace them. 'If alcopops had not been available, I very much doubt that the drinking patterns would have been different. The trend has been going up throughout the Nineties, even before alcopops,' she said.

The survey found that between 1990 and 1996, the average intake among those aged between 11 and 15 in England doubled from the equivalent of just under half a pint of beer a week to nearly a pint. One in 20 boys and one in 30 girls was drinking more than a pint a day.

Alcohol Concern said the report showed that alcopops were part of a worrying trend of under-age drinking but were not the sole cause.

The Portman Group, representing drinks manufacturers, said the survey confirmed its findings that most teenagers 'drink only occasionally and moderately'.

© Telegraph Group Limited, London 1998

It all adds up

The sensible drinking guidelines explained

This information is based on the Government's guidelines.[1] Most people enjoy drinking and find it a sociable and relaxing thing to do. Normally it leads to no harm. But there are times when drinking too much – or even drinking at all – can cause problems. For example:

Don't . . .
- drink and drive
- operate machinery, use electrical equipment or work at heights after drinking
- drink before playing sport or swimming
- drink while on certain medications – check labels and ask a doctor if unsure
- binge drink – it can lead to health and other problems.

Do . . .
- abstain for 48 hours, if you do have a episode of heavy drinking, to let your body recover
- remember drinks poured at home are often bigger than pub measures
- work out how much you drink and try to stick to the guidelines – which are daily benchmarks not weekly targets
- get help from a doctor or a specialist agency if worried about your drinking
- remember that drinking responsibly can be enjoyable and is compatible with a healthy lifestyle.

Women and men
- Most women can drink up to two to three units of alcohol a day without significant risk to their health.
- Women who are trying to conceive or who are pregnant should avoid getting drunk and are advised to consume no more than one to two units of alcohol once or twice a week.
- After the menopause there is evidence that drinking one to two pints a day, but no more, can protect against the risk of coronary heart disease.
- Most men can drink up to three to four units of alcohol a day without significant risks to their health.
- For men aged 40 and over there is evidence that drinking one or two units a day, but no more, can reduce the risk of coronary heart disease.

20

Know the score

Beer, lager and cider
330ml bottle at 4% or 5% ABV = 1.5 units
440ml can at 4% or 5% ABV = 2 units
440ml can at 8% or 9% ABV = 3.5 to 4 units
500ml can at 8% or 9% ABV = 4 to 4.5 units

Low alcohol beer and lager
440 ml can at 1.2% ABV = 0.5 units

Wine
125ml glass of wine at 11% or 12% ABV = 1.5 units
175ml glass of wine at 11% or 12% ABV = 2 units

Spirits
25ml measure of spirit at 40% ABV = 1 unit

Sherry, port, madeira and vermouth
50ml measure at 20% ABV = 1 unit

Alcopops
330ml bottle at 4% to 6% ABV = between 1.5 and 2 units
200ml bottle at 13.5% ABV = 2.5 units

One unit of pure alcohol = about half a pint (284ml) of ordinary strength lager, beer or cider, typically 3.5% alcohol by volume (ABV); a 25ml pub measure of spirit, typically 40% ABV; a small glass of 9% ABV wine.

Some drinks are stronger than others. For example a pint of premium lager has more units of alcohol in it than a standard-strength beer. And most bottles of wine are 11% or 12% ABV. You can work out the number of units in a drink by multiplying the volume in ml by the percentage ABV and dividing the total by 1,000. This guide may look complicated but with so many different sizes of glasses, cans and bottles and variations in strengths of drink, you need to make sure that you get your units right. The figures listed are rounded to the nearest half unit.

References
1. *Sensible Drinking*, the report of an Inter-Departmental working group, published in December 1995.

The sensible drinking quiz

Test your knowledge of the Government's sensible-drinking guidelines. Answers below.

1) *One unit of alcohol is defined as:*
    0.08g   0.8g   8g   8.8g

2) *One unit is equivalent to the amount of alcohol in how much standard-strength beer?*
    33cl   1/2 pint   1 pint   75cl

3) *The most common standard pub measure for spirits is:*
    2.5ml   25ml   25cl   250ml

4) *Up to how many units a day can most men regularly drink without significant health risks?*
    1 to 2   2 to 3   3 to 4   4 to 5

5) *Up to how many units a day can most women regularly drink without significant health risks?*
    1 to 2   2 to 3   3 to 4   4 to 5

6) *In pregnancy, women are advised to drink no more than one to two units:*
    every day   once a week   twice a week   once or twice a week

7) *Men over 40 and post-menopausal women can consider drinking up to how many unit(s) a day for positive health benefits?*
    Up to 1   1   between 1 and 2   between 2 and 3

8) *If you heavily exceed the guidelines on a particular day, for how long should you abstain to recover?*
    12 hours   24 hours   36 hours   48 hours

Quiz answers
1) 8g, **2)** ¹/₂ pint, **3)** 25ml, **4)** 3 to 4, **5)** 2 to 3, **6)** once or twice a week, **7)** between 1 and 2, **8)** 48hrs

• The above is an extract from *It all adds up*, produced by The Portman Group. See page 41 for address details.

Under the influence

Coping with parents who drink too much. A report on the needs of children of problem drinking parents. By Toni Brisby, Sue Baker and Teresa Hedderwick

Introduction

Children whose parents drink too much are children at risk. They are at risk of physical and emotional neglect or abuse, of unhappy, stressful childhoods and of serious problems in adult life. This report produced by Alcohol Concern examines the effects of parents' drinking and calls for action to provide services for a group of children who up to this time have been very much neglected.

Numbers of children affected

With approximately 13.5 million parents in the UK, of whom 7% will be drinking at harmful levels (35 and 50 units and above for women and men respectively), and with a similar number of under-18s, 920,000 children in the UK could be living in a family where a parent has an alcohol problem.

What the research shows

The most common effects of problem drinking are arguments and family conflict. This more than anything else does harm to children, producing damage that can last into adult life. Young people in families with a drinking parent have rates of psychiatric disorder at the age of 15 between 2.2 to 3.9 times higher than other young people.

Violence, child abuse and family breakdown are all associated with alcohol problems. Alcohol is a factor in a third of child abuse cases and 40% of domestic violence incidents. Twice as many alcohol-complicated marriages end in divorce than marriages where there are no alcohol problems.

The research also points to ways of reducing the short-term suffering and long-term damage to children. Children seem to survive quite well as long as the level of family conflict is low, parents enforce family rules in a reasonably consistent way and there is some sort of regular pattern to life. They also benefit if the drinker acknowledges that it is his or her problem and not the children who are to blame.

How children feel

Living with a problem drinking parent is very difficult for children. It can take away a young person's childhood, forcing them to shoulder responsibilities far beyond what could be expected. The ordinary routines of family life are fraught with difficulties because drinkers tend to behave in unpredictable ways, often swinging wildly between being aggressive and violent, silently withdrawn, or talkative and emotional.

Celebrating major events like birthdays often becomes impossible. Coming home from school can be frightening, because children never know what they will find. Many have seen their parent unconscious, injured and bleeding, vomiting, or incontinent and have had to deal with these situations.

Often children feel guilty and to blame, believing that if they were better behaved or more successful their parent would have no need to drink. Some children become difficult and unruly, some withdraw into themselves. Virtually all children whose parents have an alcohol problem feel lonely and 'switched off', both from relationships within their family and with other people, in particular because families often work very hard to keep problem drinking a secret from the rest of the world.

What is being done now to provide help

Alcohol Concern asked alcohol services and other organisations throughout England and Wales about what they provide for children of problem drinking parents.

The study found that there was very little help available for this group of children. Specialist alcohol

services often have no tradition of working with young people and many expressly exclude children, although a small number of agencies are starting to employ specialist young people's workers and some provide family services. In a very small number of cases there is a service specifically designed for parents and for children of problem drinking parents.

However, only a minority of people with alcohol problems actually approach specialist services for help with their drinking. Teachers, medical and nursing staff, social workers, the police, young people's counselling services and a whole range of other professions encounter children suffering because a parent has an alcohol problem, but on the whole they are not well equipped to recognise, or respond to, this problem.

Why there is so little provision

The way society deals with alcohol is often unhelpful and inconsistent.

When a parent is found to be using illegal drugs, the family is very likely to be seen as one which needs help. When the issue is alcohol, the situation is likely to be ignored or treated with amused tolerance until the family hits a crisis. Added to this are the facts that families with alcohol problems have powerful reasons for keeping it secret, specialist services are often not funded or trained to provide for children and general childcare and family services are rarely trained in managing alcohol problems.

What should be done

The evidence shows that these children are children in need. Because of this, all agencies who come into contact with children or parents must be seen as having a responsibility to protect and support them and to do this without increasing the stigma that is already attached to alcohol problems. In particular, the objective should be to provide support to help parents to function better and to remove from children the fear that the family will be split up unless there is absolutely no alternative.

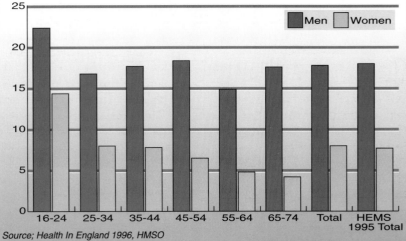

Weekly consumption

This survey shows that women's consumption of alcohol was much lower than men's: the mean weekly number of units consumed by women was 7.7 compared with 18.0 for men. The graph below shows the mean weekly consumption of alcohol in units by age: adults aged 16-74.

Source; Health In England 1996, HMSO

Given the lack of information about the total extent of the problem, the lack of collaboration on this issue and the absence of models of interventions aimed at this group, key organisations concerned with the provision of care to children should come together to identify specific actions required locally, the information needs of planners and commissioners, to identify possible pilot projects and to develop planning and practice guidance. The Government has a central role in ensuring appropriate organisations can work together and in ensuring that the many planning systems already in place to provide services are fully equipped to take account of the needs of children of problem drinking parents. However immediate action can, and should, be taken. In particular the Government should require that the needs of these children are addressed in Children's Services Plans and Community Care Plans. It should give specific guidance on how local service providers should view their obligations under children's legislation and, where necessary, ensure that resources are available to respond to identified needs.

When the issue is alcohol, the situation is likely to be ignored

---

At local level there is an urgent need for intensive awareness raising and training so that everyone, including doctors, nurses, teachers, social workers, lawyers and the police, through to the many workers who come into contact with children and families on a less formal basis, are competent to take account of the needs of children whenever adult drinking is identified. Alongside this the specialist alcohol services (and their funders) should be encouraged to develop their role in supporting other professionals and in working in partnership with other agencies to assist clients who are parents.

Finally, counselling and other services for children and families, which are easy to access and which can deal properly with children's need for confidentiality, should be available locally throughout the British Isles. The voluntary sector has a central role to play here.

The overarching recommendation, which must be the responsibility of Government, is that the only way forward is for planners, commissioning organisations, alcohol services and children's service providers to co-operate together to meet the needs of this group.

• The above is an extract from a 40-page report available from the Alcohol Concern Bookshop under the category of N. Social effects/crime. See page 41 for address details.
© *Alcohol Concern*

Could red wine really do more good than harm?

How good is it for you?

For years we've been told to cut down on alcohol to enable us to lead healthier lives. But tell French or Italians that cutting out red wine can help you to live longer, and you'll be laughed out of the restaurant.

So what is the truth? Is red wine bad for them, or does it contain nutrients and compounds that really can improve our well-being?

For years, many doctors have held the belief that red wine does have medicinal qualities. It is credited with easing stress, lowering deaths from cardiovascular disease and even reducing the risk of Alzheimer's – cause enough for celebration with a glass of good claret.

But before you reach for the corkscrew, are the claims based on science or merely on wishful thinking?

It is proved beyond doubt that people consuming regular, moderate amounts of alcohol – about two or three small glasses a day – have a lower risk of coronary heart disease than either teetotallers or heavy drinkers. And although wine has received by far the most attention for its health benefits, a cardio-protective effect can be also shown for beer and spirit drinkers, too.

Alcohol reduces the stickiness of the blood and helps steer cholesterol away from blood vessel walls.

But younger drinkers cannot store up benefit for later years. 'A moderate alcohol intake only confers protection on men over 40 and post-menopausal women,' says Gary Ward of the Health Education Authority's alcohol project. 'The emphasis is on regular, moderate amounts. The concept falls down if you consistently over-indulge or have a weekly binge.'

Where red wine may score more highly than other alcoholic drinks is in its extra ingredients. Substances called flavonoids which give red wine its colour are also found in fruits and vegetables.

'There is mounting evidence to point to the flavonoids as being important contributory factors in the prevention of heart disease,' says Professor Catherine Rice-Evans, of the United Medical and Dental Schools of Guy's and St Thomas's Hospitals, London.

Four glasses of wine a day is at the top end of safe alcohol intake for men, and above it for women

---

'They might be acting as anti-oxidants and they may also be preventing certain cells in the blood from clumping together and causing a blockage.

'Drinking your red wine with a healthy meal could also mean that the beneficial components you are eating get absorbed better.'

So far, so good. But surely drinking wine makes you fat? Not necessarily, says Professor Loren Cordain, from the Department of Exercise and Sport Science at Colorado State University. His team monitored body weight variables in 14 healthy men, average age 30, over a 12-week period.

The men were asked to drink two 135ml glasses of red wine a day with their evening meal for six weeks and then have no alcohol for six weeks.

The results of the study, published in last month's *Journal of the American College of Nutrition* and partly funded by the Wine Institute, showed no tendency for the men to put on weight even though the wine was in addition to normal food intake.

But Helen Lloyd, a scientist at the British Nutrition Foundation, says: 'Two hundred calories from a couple of glasses of red wine might make little difference if you are sensible about what you eat. But if they are more than your needs, you will put on weight.'

The *Neurological Review* re-ports on a nine-year study by scientists at Bordeaux University who investigated the drinking habits of nearly 4,000 people over 65 and concluded that an intake of four glasses of wine a day reduced the risk of developing Alzheimer's disease by 75 per cent. Lower or higher intakes did not have the same benefit.

While welcoming research into the condition, the Alzheimer's Disease Society remains sceptical. 'Alzheimer's is a very emotive issue,' says spokeswoman Veronica Fuller. 'People might like to think that drinking red wine will prevent senility, but this is just one study. There are many more that show alcohol can kill brain cells.'

The Health Education Authority points out that four glasses of wine a day is at the top end of safe alcohol intake for men, and above it for women. And the dangers of alcohol in excess – red wine or not – can far outweigh the benefits it might otherwise provide.

Drink and be damned

Why are women constantly lectured about their alcohol consumption? Kate Taylor stands up for boozy floozies

So recent research has revealed that women who drink as little as five glasses of wine a week can drastically reduce their chances of getting pregnant. Well, excuse me if this column looks rushed, but I'm just out to invest in three cases. Like many women of my age, my biological clock is firmly on snooze and the only dribbling infant I want around the place is my boyfriend. But the fact that this research, by doctors in Denmark, was plastered (or rather, not) across the papers last week, and not given only to pregnancy magazines, where it might reach relevant readers, suggests to me that this report is an example of a worrying trend: women are simply not allowed to get drunk.

Let's face it: any woman who seriously wanted to conceive would lay off the lagers. For one thing, we're in touch with our bodies enough to twig that downing milk and vitamins is more likely to help our ovaries kick in than necking Chianti. With alcohol, as with all other areas of our lives, women are perfectly adept at making the right choices for ourselves, ta very much. But once again the world is full of father figures trying to call time on our fun.

It's always been the same. In the first public houses, the only time a woman was allowed to appear was as a worried figure at the door telling her husband the farm had burned down. In the saloon bars of the Wild West, prostitutes were allowed to visit only as attractions laid on (literally) by the landlord. As recently as this century, drawing-rooms were invented as places for women to push-off to while the men downed port, and in modern-day America, a new law has been introduced to lock up pregnant women who might have a drink problem. (Their husbands, of course, can remain more pickled than the last onion in the jar.)

But bearing in mind that the majority of alcohol-influenced crimes – from drunk-driving to wife-beating – are committed by men, why are we the ones to bear the brunt of alcohol-safety announcements?

Apparently, the women most likely to drink more than the recommended one spritzer every other year are aged 20-25 and in full-time employment. It's here, experts say, that females are more likely to drink 'to keep up with their male colleagues'. Er, hello? Excuse me while I spill my pint in shock, but that is so wrong. Her male colleagues – and their behaviour while drunk – are probably the most discouraging advert for alcohol a woman can find.

Far from turning into the friendly, likeable laugh that women can become half-way down a bottle of Chateau Rouge, a bloke on a bender can be transformed into a dangerous, introspective nightmare after just three rounds. Women are far better at holding their booze than men, mainly because we know when to stop. Look at the Ulrika Jonsson/ Stan Collymore incident that so many papers leapt on.

'Pint-drinking Ulrika is the role model for the new Ladettes,' the tabloids jeered. Yeah, but it wasn't her knocking old Collymore around when he didn't want to go home was it? Women are safer under the influence. And to any man that disagrees with this statement, I'd just ask one question: who would you rather find yourself next to in a night-club – a gaggle of bevved-up beauties out on a hen-night, or a growling, prowling pack of drunken stag-nighters? With both of them, you might not wake up at home the next morning, but at least with the women it won't be in hospital.

Hopefully, things will start improving for women who like a drink. As breweries recognise the oestrogen economy, we'll start seeing more drinks aimed at our tastes, and less statistics aimed at frightening us out of the snug. More money will be spent on targeting male alcohol abusers while we can get on with getting under the table. The new range of All Bar One-style female-friendly pubs will expand, and soon we might even be allowed to consume more than half a glass of Pinot Noir without feeling that the whole of the next generation is coming under threat.

And when we're finally allowed to indulge ourselves, we can look forward to waking up feeling okay. We might never have a clear head, but at least we'll have a clear conscience. Cheers. *© The Guardian August, 1998*

EXPECTING MY FIRST BEER GUT!

Condon links drink to rise in violence

By Jason Bennetto, Crime Correspondent

Britain's senior police chief yesterday blamed excessive drinking among the young for the rise in violent crime.

Sir Paul Condon, the Commissioner of the Metropolitan Police, in an interview with *The Independent*, said the nation-wide problem of rising violence was linked to young people having more money for alcohol and a greater choice of places to drink. He also blamed the drug and rave culture.

There is growing concern over casual and unprovoked assaults. The number of violent crimes recorded by the police have increased every year for the past decade. Violent offences in Greater Manchester rose by 50 per cent in the past year, according to figures released last week.

Sir Paul said: 'Where I think there has been a real increase is violence between young people linked to drink. That's where the growth is. It is about affluence, relative affluence of young people, their ability to drink and club. There are influences from the drugs and rave culture.

'Lifestyle changes have encouraged violence in those sort of circumstances. There are more venues to go to.'

The Home Office's chief criminologist has also expressed his fears about violent crime that is linked to alcohol, which rose to 350,700 offences in England and Wales in 1997 – it makes up 8 per cent of all crime. The marketing of extra strong alcoholic drinks aimed at the young has also been identified as an influence.

The Home Office is at present reviewing the licensing laws and a coalition group of police, magistrates, brewers and local authorities yesterday claimed to be gaining support for new legislation to allow all-night drinking by 2000.

In London, while overall crime has declined in the past year, violent offences rose by 6 per cent. Sir Paul said it was often hard to tackle violent offences because they usually take place behind closed doors.

> ### The marketing of extra strong alcoholic drinks aimed at the young has also been identified as an influence

Among the techniques being considered by Scotland Yard are 'naming and shaming' pubs and clubs in the media and installing surveillance cameras at trouble spots. He revealed that Scotland Yard has drawn up extensive plans to deal with any violence or mass disturbances at the thousands of pubs and clubs in London planning to screen World Cup football.

Another reason for the rise in recorded violent offences is, Sir Paul believes, improved reporting and more sympathetic treatment of victims, particularly those of domestic violence and child abuse. Sir Paul also disclosed that the Metropolitan Police had set up an inquiry into why black people are far more likely than whites to be stopped and searched in the capital.

The commissioner defended the use of his force's stop-and-search practices, arguing that when the police tactic was reduced by half in a racially sensitive area of north London, the number of reported crimes increased by one-third.

The comments follow an unpublished report, revealed in *The Independent*, which showed police in London stopped and searched 4.5 black people and 1.3 Asians for every white person, proportionate to population.

Research into the use of stop-and-search is at present being carried out at five pilot areas, including Tottenham in north London. Sir Paul explained: 'We need to understand why young black men are disproportionately stopped.'

© *The Independent*
June, 1998

Doctors dispute drop in drink-related violence

Cutting late-night opening hours of pubs and clubs does not mean less alcohol-related city-centre violence, according to a study by accident and emergency unit doctors.

The research, which has sparked a row with police, showed assaults in the city of Edinburgh did not fall when extensions to licensing hours were restricted, despite police crime figures to the contrary. The research, carried out on behalf of the *British Medical Journal* at the accident and emergency department of Edinburgh Royal Infirmary, took place during the weeks immediately before and after the licensing restrictions were put in place in March 1996.

Staggered closing hours, which dated from 1990, were replaced with a uniform curfew of 1am which was designed to cut out late night roaming of gangs of youths intent on finding bars that remained open until 2am and 3am.

Dr Colin Graham who is now based at Inverclyde Royal Hospital said: 'The research may have been carried out at one accident and emergency department but the findings are reflected across the rest of the country.

'Basically it does not matter how you arrange licensing hours. If there is to be a fall in the number of those presenting at casualty departments something has to be done about the whole culture of drinking rather than the hours at which you allow it to take place in a pub.

'They don't make a difference at all and this is a massive problem for hospitals who have to spend valuable time dealing with drunk and abusive patients.'

However the figures and the conclusions have been criticised by Lothian and Borders police. Inspector Douglas Muir, the officer in charge of licensing for the force, said: 'I cannot believe these figures. They are complete fiction. It was not a complete survey because almost half of those who attended the accident and emergency department during the study period were not tested. You have to have the whole facts before you and they do not.'

'We have figures to show that violent assaults carried out during that period fell sharply because of the change in the licensing hours'

He added: 'We have figures to show that violent assaults carried out during that period fell sharply because of the change in the licensing hours.' Of the 5,023 patients seen in the accident and emergency department during three study periods, 2,187 (43.5 per cent) failed to provide a breath sample, either because they could or would not take the test, or because the department was too busy.

Edinburgh's licensing board convener, Dougie Kerr, said: 'I would be interested to read this report because it does not accord with what the police are telling us.

'Since we introduced a uniform policy of 1am opening for public houses and 3am for clubs the police say there has been a definite reduction in the number of late-night incidents the police are having to deal with.

'The police report regularly to the board and we are constantly reviewing our policy on late-night opening, but it does appear that we have now struck the proper balance which allows Edinburgh as a major tourist destination to have later opening hours than other cities without harming the interests of residents.'

Mr Kerr said: 'We will not hesitate to use this measure again. Usually if we suspend the licence of a person whose premises are involved in violence, they simply go to court and that, at the very least, delays the action against them.

'Cutting the hours that premises are allowed to open is a reasonable way of immediately punishing those who do not fulfil their responsibilities.'

© *The Scotsman*
January, 1998

I'D BUY ME A DRINK IF I WERE YOU—I GET AGGRESSIVE WHEN I'M SOBER!

Move to reduce alcohol limit in drive to cut road deaths

Drinking and driving claims the lives of more than 500 people every year. Randeep Ramesh and Jeremy Riggall examine the measures ministers are considering to cut the death toll on Britain's roads

The Government is to launch a consultation paper at the end of this month which will propose a lower drink-driving limit and set out radical measures to deter motorists from drinking and driving.

Ministers favour a blood alcohol limit of 50 milligrams of alcohol per 100 per millilitres of blood – down from the present 80mg limit. It will be the first reduction in 30 years. The year-long driving ban is likely to stay.

Any reduction is unlikely to produce a backlash. A recent poll by ICM showed 85 per cent of the public backed a lowering of the limit.

Although Britain is recognised as having an effective road safety policy, officials say the number of deaths caused by drink-driving has remained static at 540 a year for four years.

In order to cut further the death toll, ministers are minded to consider tougher penalties for high-risk or repeat offenders. These measures may see persistent offenders losing their licences for life or extend the mandatory 12-month driving ban. Another option could see motorists who ignore the drink-driving limit forfeiting their car.

Young drivers may also face tougher drink-drive limits. Officials point out although 'early' drivers only make up 10 per cent of the driving population, they cause 20 per cent of accidents. In some US states, the number of fatalities caused by young drivers dropped by 50 per cent after introducing 'super-low' limits for teenagers.

Ministers, however, have been advised that a limit of 20mg for motorists with less than three years' driving experience may not significantly cut accident rates. Civil servants say creating a two-tier system may just result in young drivers drinking more after they pass a certain date.

Motoring organisations are not in favour of tougher drink-drive limits. 'We think more police enforcement of the current limits would significantly bring down levels,' said a spokesman for the AA.

But evidence suggests otherwise. Experts say that having 50mg of alcohol in 100ml of blood makes a driver twice as likely to have an accident as a motorist with a zero reading. Researchers at the University of Leeds have shown that despite being under the current limit, motorists' driving can be affected. 'There are small but consistent detriments to driving even under 80mg,' said Andrew Parks, principal research fellow.

Richard Allsop, professor of transport studies at University College, London, estimates that 100 lives a year could be saved if the 50mg limit was adopted. Random breath testing by the Department of Environment, Transport and the Regions showed 2.3 per cent of drivers could be driving with alcohol levels between 40mg and 80mg.

A lower limit will bring Britain in line with the rest of Europe. France, Belgium, Greece and the Netherlands all have a 50mg limit.

Sweden has the lowest drink-driving laws, set at 20mg in 1990. 'From January to the end of October we carried out 12,000 alcohol tests and found only 90 to be above 20mg, which works out at 0.75 per cent,' said inspector Glenn Andersson of Stockholm police.

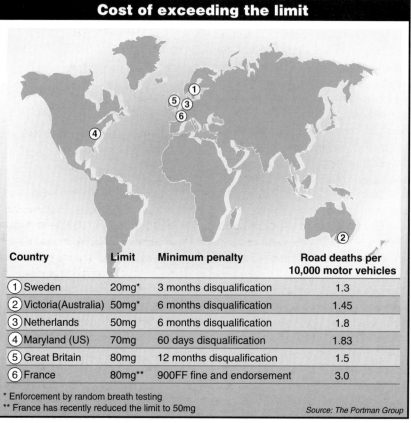

Cost of exceeding the limit

Country	Limit	Minimum penalty	Road deaths per 10,000 motor vehicles
① Sweden	20mg*	3 months disqualification	1.3
② Victoria(Australia)	50mg*	6 months disqualification	1.45
③ Netherlands	50mg	6 months disqualification	1.8
④ Maryland (US)	70mg	60 days disqualification	1.83
⑤ Great Britain	80mg	12 months disqualification	1.5
⑥ France	80mg**	900FF fine and endorsement	3.0

* Enforcement by random breath testing
** France has recently reduced the limit to 50mg

Source: The Portman Group

With twice as many road deaths as Britain, France lowered its limit to 50mg in 1995 and introduced campaigns to inform people how much they could drink. Disposable breathalysers were put on sale in service stations, supermarkets and chemists. Initial reports claim this has saved lives.

Paul Dumontet, spokesman for the transport department in France, says that having a glass or two with a meal is *de rigueur* for the French. 'We have to be realistic. The French like to drink wine at lunch time. We are simply trying what the safe driving alcohol level is.'

British ministers believe the problem with countries such as Belgium and France is not the limit, but the very light penalties.

At Westminster, ministers are keen to promote a package of measures. Reducing the alcohol limit has to go hand in hand with enforcement to get results. When politicians in the Capital Territory of Australia reduced the limit from 80mg to 50mg they also introduced random breath testing, and there was a 41 per cent reduction in offenders who were three times over the limit.

'We aim to cut the number of deaths on Britain's roads significantly,' said Baroness Hayman last week. 'But we will do so with a balanced package. There are many weapons in the armoury. But it will be through education first, then compliance, enforcement and finally legislation that we bring about change.'

© The Independent
January, 1998

Ignorance over drink levels

By David Brindle, Social Services Correspondent

Only one in five men and fewer than one in three women know how much they ought safely to drink.

More than two in three people either do not know the limit or think it higher than it is, according to the survey of more than 3,600 men and women by the Office for National Statistics.

The findings confirm widespread confusion about 'safe' drinking limits since the Department of Health two years ago dropped the previous figures advising maximum weekly consumption.

The new guidance states that for men, consistently drinking four or more units of alcohol a day is not recommended. For women, the equivalent figure is three units a day. A unit is a half-pint of beer, glass of wine or single measure of spirits.

Of those taking part in the survey, carried out in February and March, only 20 per cent of men thought three units the safe daily limit for them. Another 8 per cent thought it was less, 33 per cent more and 38 per cent did not know.

Similarly, 28 per cent of women believed two units was their safe daily limit, 4 per cent thought it less, 24 per cent more and 43 per cent did not know.

The Department of Health said the Government was reassessing all its advice on healthy diet as part of the health promotion review.

The charity Alcohol Concern called for a greatly increased campaign on the risks of excess drinking. The charity, which expects more than 10,000 people a day to seek help with drink-related problems over Christmas, wants the Government to tax alcohol advertisers to fund more intensive health education.

Seven in 10 men and almost six in 10 women say they drink at least once a week, says the ONS survey. Ten per cent of men and 6 per cent of women admit to drinking every day.

Asked how often they got 'at least slightly drunk' 8 per cent of men and 3 per cent of women said every week – although half all men and two in three women said never.

In the 16-24 age group, the proportion of men who admitted getting at least slightly drunk every week rose to almost one in five.

• *Drinking: Adults' Behaviour and Knowledge*; Stationery Office, £10.95

© The Guardian
December, 1997

Drinking and driving

Percentage of drivers and riders killed in GB, whose blood alcohol level was known, who were over the legal limit:

Convictions for alcohol-related driving offences:

1989	1990	1991	1992	1993	1994	1995
114,000	113,000	104,000	95,000	91,000	90,000	93,000

Source: Department of the Environment, Transport and the Regions, September 1997

Alcohol tops problems in casualty

As many as eight in 10 people being treated by hospital casualty departments at any one time have alcohol-related injuries or problems, says a study published today.

Even children's hospitals have to deal with cases involving excess alcohol consumption, the research found. One reported a child admitted after sipping vodka and blackcurrant juice from a flask throughout the school day.

The study, by the Health Education Authority, involved a survey of 80 per cent of the 224 general accident and emergency departments in England to establish what action casualty staff took to help people with problem drinking.

It also involved discussion groups with doctors and nurses in casualty departments in hospitals in Bristol, Weston-super-Mare and Southampton.

On average through the week, one patient in six was thought to have an alcohol-related condition. However, the research teams from Imperial College, London, and the University of Wales felt the true incidence could be higher because of a general lack of procedures to monitor and record patients' sobriety.

On Friday and Saturday nights, the hospitals reported, as many as 80 per cent of patients would have a drink-related injury or problem.

One health worker told the researchers: 'Sometimes we get runs where 98 to 100 per cent are alcohol-related in a block of time.'

The survey found that people attending casualty with an alcohol-related condition were more than twice as likely to arrive by ambulance. One in three had been involved in an assault.

Other conditions included alcohol withdrawal symptoms, self-injury, alcohol poisoning, road accidents and accidents at home.

Of 47 cases studied at Bristol children's hospital, 42 involved patients aged 13-16. One staff member said: 'The ones that actually come in have usually passed out in the street or at a party.'

The HEA is developing schemes to help casualty staff respond more effectively to patients with alcohol-related conditions, encouraging them to deal with the issue rather than simply patching them up.

Lynne Friedli, the authority's alcohol programme manager, said the aim was to reduce the number of people making return visits. 'The problems faced by doctors and nurses are far removed from the trendy image of alcohol promoted by advertising.'

Some staff were doubtful they could achieve much, estimating that only 20-30 per cent of the patients concerned were sober enough to take in advice.

© The Guardian
March, 1998

Drinking and driving

- Drink-driving has dropped dramatically over the past ten years. Drink-drive fatalities were 990 in 1986, compared with 540 (provisional) for 1996. However this is 15% of total deaths, which is still too high.
- In 1996 159,000 drivers and riders in road injury accidents were breath tested, with a 5.1% failure rate, which compares very favourably with 61,000 drivers and riders being breath tested in 1986 with a 19.5% failure rate.

Key changes in behaviour and attitudes 1979-1997

Research carried out for the Department between 1979 and 1997 shows significant changes in drinking and driving behaviour since the campaign began in the late 1970s.

The research was carried out amongst men who drive and also drink outside the home.

- In 1979, 51% had driven after drinking on at least one occasion in the last week, by 1997 this had fallen to 23%.
- Over the same period the proportion drinking 6+ units and then driving on at least one occasion in the last week fell from 15% to 3%.
- The proportion claiming to 'leave the car at home when going drinking' has increased from 54% to 79% and the proportion claiming to avoid the risk by 'arranging for someone else to drive' has also increased from 48% to 67%.

Key facts

- In 1995 38% of drink-drive accidents involved only one vehicle compared with 14% for all accidents.
- Of the 540 deaths in drink-drive accidents in 1995, 56% were drivers or riders over the limit and 44% innocent victims.
- 2360 car drivers and passengers of all ages were seriously injured. Of these 990 were drivers over the limit and 310 under the limit. 1050 were passengers.

© Department of the Environment,
Transport and the Regions,
September, 1998

Drink-drive plan is shelved as EU stops interfering

By Toby Helm, EU Correspondent in Brussels

Plans for tough EU drink-drive laws that would have almost halved the legal alcohol limit for British drivers have been shelved by Neil Kinnock, Europe's transport commissioner.

He accepted that pushing for a new Euro-law would conflict with efforts by Tony Blair and other EU leaders to curb interference from Brussels in areas that can be left to national governments.

The move is proof of growing sensitivity in the Brussels Commission to charges of meddling. It comes as heads of government prepare for next month's EU summit on how to make Europe more relevant to ordinary people.

Mr Kinnock proposed the new laws after a survey showing that 45,000 people are killed each year on Europe's roads, many in alcohol-related accidents. He planned to set a legal alcohol limit for all drivers in Europe of 50 milligrams per 100 millilitres of blood.

The current limit in Britain is 80 mg – the equivalent of about two pints of beer or two and a half glasses of wine.

The new rules would have meant that anyone drinking more than a pint of beer or one and a half glasses of wine would have been at risk of prosecution.

Several EU governments, including Britain, doubted whether action at European level was the way forward.

In February, British transport ministers issued their own consultation document aimed at establishing whether a change in UK law would work. But Britain's six-month presidency of the EU, which ended on June 30, conspicuously failed to advance Mr Kinnock's plan.

Officials in the Commission said Mr Kinnock was happy to have contributed to a debate on the issue.

They added that a push for EU legislation would not look good at a time when governments were trying to flesh out ideas on how to apply 'subsidiarity' – the principle that decisions should be taken at national level wherever possible.

The new rules would have meant that anyone drinking more than a pint of beer would have been at risk of prosecution

---

Although motoring organisations have welcomed Mr Kinnock's commitment to road safety, some expressed doubts about the effectiveness of a uniform limit.

The RAC described the EU proposals, which were originally put forward in 1988 before being revived last year by Mr Kinnock, as a 'bit of a red herring'. It said the main challenge was to catch a hard core of offenders who regularly exceeded the limit by large amounts.

Mr Kinnock's backdown will also please Jacques Santer, the Commission president, who has launched his own crusade to defend Brussels against charges of excessive interference.

In June, Mr Santer said he was tired of hearing Brussels being pilloried.

He said national governments were often to blame for pushing their own schemes too hard, and promised to ensure that Brussels 'does less and does it better'.

© Telegraph Group Limited, London 1998

Drink driving limits in the EU

Alcohol in the blood per 100ml

1.	Austria	50mg	9.	France	50mg
2.	Belgium	50mg	10.	Italy	80mg
3.	Denmark	80mg	11.	Luxembourg	80mg
4.	Germany	80mg	12.	Netherlands	50mg
5.	Ireland	80mg	13.	Portugal	50mg
6.	Greece	50mg	14.	Sweden	20mg
7.	Spain	80mg	15.	**UK**	**80mg**
8.	Finland	50mg			

Drink-drive payout could reach £3m

By Jason Bennetto, Crime Correspondent

More than £300,000 compensation has been paid to about 60 motorists who were wrongly convicted of drinking and driving after police tested their blood with swabs containing alcohol, it was revealed yesterday.

Up to 400 people may be entitled to damages which could cost the Home Office as much as £3m in compensation. The payouts so far range from a few thousand pounds to £25,000.

The testing fiasco is one of the worst contamination cases involving police equipment.

Solicitors representing about 70 people who have had their convictions quashed said yesterday that many of their clients have had their lives and businesses ruined by the mix-up.

The contamination took place in the Greater Manchester area between March 1987 and December 1988. It happened after police complained that the antiseptic swabs used to wipe over a motorist's arm before taking a blood sample were very old and had become too dry to use.

The police requested new swabs from the Home Office, but were unknowingly sent wipes that contained alcohol and could therefore have contaminated the blood samples. It is unclear whether the Home Office suppliers provided the wrong equipment or the police failed to ask for non-alcoholic wipes.

The Forensic Science Service discovered the mistake and all drivers found guilty during the 18-month period had their convictions quashed.

Greater Manchester police successfully defended a claim for compensation, but the Home Office admitted liability and set up an adjudicator who has authorised up to 40 payments in the past few months. Those who have received compensation include:

- Two people who attempted suicide after allegedly becoming depressed at the disgrace of being convicted of drinking and driving.

> ## Up to 400 people may be entitled to damages which could cost the Home Office as much as £3m in compensation

- A young man who was jailed for three months.
- Several people who had their photographs, names and addresses published in a local paper's 'rogues' gallery'.
- A man who owned a garage and went bust, partly because he was banned from driving.
- A person who spent a year having to cycle eight miles to a railway station to get to work.

A Home Office spokeswoman said that 58 awards had been made so far and that a further 30 were currently being considered.

A spokeswoman for Greater Manchester police added that the Home Office had supplied the faulty swabs and was paying compensation. But she refused to comment further.

Police and the Home Office are currently considering the introduction of roadside drug-testing equipment, although there is concern that kits are not sensitive enough accurately to detect illegal substances. The Manchester case illustrates another potential pitfall.

© *The Independent*
June, 1998

Police enforcement

Breath tests administered in England and Wales:

Proportion positive/refused:

1989	1990	1991	1992	1993	1994	1995	1996
20%	17%	16%	16%	15%	14%	13%	13%

Source: Department of the Environment, Transport and the Regions, September 1997

Do I have an alcohol problem?

Information from Alcohol Concern

The first thing to consider is how much you actually drink. Try to compile a drinking diary of what you had last week. Be careful to include all the drinks and remember that at home a glass of wine or spirits is often bigger than a pub measure! Was this a typical week? If you are drinking above the recommended limits you should think about cutting down.

If you are worried that drinking may be becoming a problem for you, warning signs can be:

- Being drunk more often, particularly when needing to be on good form the next day.
- Taking the day off because of a hangover.
- Having accidents, domestic arguments or injuries because of drink.
- Getting into trouble because of drinking – fights, drinking and driving.
- Doing something you would not otherwise have done after drinking and regretting it.
- Drinking more than you planned to in an evening.

If these are only isolated incidents you may just need to think more carefully about reducing the number of drinks you have and when you decide to have them. However if many of the other signs given below apply, you may be getting into a pattern of problem drinking.

- Thinking a lot about when you can next have a drink.
- Gulping your first drink quickly.
- Being conscious of how often you are the first person to finish a drink.
- Having more than the occasional hangover.
- Needing to have a drink before doing things or facing certain situations.

- Feeling sick, having the shakes, sweating in the morning or middle of the night.
- Spending more than you can afford on alcohol.
- Ordering doubles when it's your round.
- Often feeling that you need a drink.
- Increase in arguments and rows at home over drink.
- Being annoyed if others mention your drinking or your behaviour when you were drunk.
- Other people telling you that they are worried about your drinking.
- Feeling secretly uncomfortable about your drinking.
- Drinking when alone.
- Deliberately hiding the evidence of your drinking (lying about money, hiding drink and empty alcohol containers).
- Starting to drink at times when you didn't before and earlier in the day.

You are likely to have a definite problem with alcohol or have become addicted if you:

- Have to increase the amount you drink to maintain the same effect.
- Always wake up with the shakes and feeling sweaty.
- Need a drink to start the day.
- Drink large quantities over the course of the day without it making you drunk.
- Feel uncomfortable if you don't have a drink at hand.
- Lie about your drinking.
- Are covering up your drinking and the costs of it.

Tips for cutting down

First start by working out what you drink in a week by reviewing the last week. If it is difficult to remember keep a daily note for the next week. Note all the drinks, how many units in each, the times of day and where you were. If this is a typical week, your notes should give you a good

idea about whether you are drinking too much and, importantly, the situations in which you drink and whether it's going to be hard to cut down.

Some things that others have found useful for cutting down include:

- Going out a bit later or just having your first drink later.
- Replacing some of your drinks with non-alcoholic or low alcohol drinks.
- Switching your usual drink to one with less alcohol in it.
- Avoiding the quick drink situation – missing out the one at lunch time or after work can make a huge difference over the week.
- Having at least two alcohol-free days – taking up a new interest, sport or just going to the cinema if you find most of your social life is involved around the pub.
- Drinking longer drinks – beer rather than spirits and drinking more slowly.
- If you drink at home, buying beers and wines with lower alcohol content could make a great difference.
- Decide a limit of no more than, say, 5 units on any one occasion.
- Buy smaller glasses for the home or buy a drinks measure.
- Keep a supply of non-alcoholic alternatives for drinking at home and entertaining.
- Tell others you are cutting down and avoid rounds.
- Finding other ways of relaxing – exercise or relaxation techniques for example.
- If you anticipate a heavy evening, avoid drinking on an empty stomach and make sure someone else is driving.

If you are worried about your drinking, are finding it hard to cut down or stop, there are many agencies which offer a confidential service and will be happy to help you.

To find your nearest local service visit the Alcohol Services Directory section, within the Alcohol Concern web site, which maintains a geographical listing of agencies in England & Wales. See page 43 for details.

© Alcohol Concern

Help for alcohol problems

Information from Alcohol Concern

The symptoms of problem drinking are described here for those who are worried about their own drinking – or maybe that of a partner, friend or relative. There are tips on cutting down and advice on seeking help. If you are worried about your health or someone else's, you should seek advice from a general practitioner.

Immediate effects of drinking

Alcohol is a drug. Its immediate effect is to alter mood. Because drinking makes people feel relaxed, happy and even euphoric, many find it surprising to learn that alcohol is in fact a depressant. As such it switches off the part of the brain which controls judgement leading to loss of inhibitions. As most people are aware, alcohol also affects physical co-ordination. The more drinks you have the greater the effect – speech becomes slurred, vision blurred, balance is lost and movements are clumsy. Heavy drinking will depress all bodily functions, so drinking very large quantities can result in un-consciousness, coma, or even death. Vomiting while unconscious or in a heavy sleep can cause death by asphyxiation.

Some people are more vulnerable to the immediate effects of alcohol depending on:

- *Body size* – because there is more blood in a large person than in a small person, the concentration of alcohol in the big person will rise more slowly, and reach a lower level, than in a small person, even if they both drink the same amount.
- *Gender* – women's bodies have more fat and less fluid than men's; so even if they are a similar size and weight to a man, and drinking the same amount, the con-centration of alcohol in the blood will be higher in the women. Women are more sensitive to the immediate effects of drinking during ovulation (about 2 weeks before a period) and in the 2 or 3 days before a period. They are likely to feel the effects of alcohol more quickly at these times than they would normally. Women using the contraceptive pill do not experience this effect, but alcohol may take longer to process.
- *Age* – it appears that both young people and older people may process alcohol more slowly, and so they will have alcohol in their systems for longer.
- *Genetics* – there may be varia-tions in how alcohol affects people of different races. For instance, many people of East Asian origin have an enzyme which causes a strong allergy-like reaction to alcohol.

Other factors which can vary the effects of alcohol are:

- *Eating before drinking* – alcohol is absorbed more quickly on an empty stomach – hence the expression 'that drink's gone straight to my head'.
- *The type of drink* – some drinks are absorbed faster than others, and so their effects are felt more quickly. Wines and sherries are absorbed more quickly than neat spirits or beers; the chemicals in sparkling wines, in lagers and in fizzy mixers speed up alcohol absorption; the sugar in sweet drinks slows it down.

Although these effects are short-term, being 'under the influence' puts you at a higher risk of accidents and can cause friction in relationships with colleagues, family and friends.

How long do the effects last?

Apart from cases of extreme intoxication, these effects are short-term.

It is the liver which breaks down and eliminates alcohol from the body, and it takes it about an hour to deal with one unit (half a pint of beer, a small glass of wine or a pub measure of spirits). So it would take the body eight hours to eliminate all the alcohol in four pints of beer. It is important to remember this if you are planning to drive – a couple of pints at lunchtime might mean your driving is still impaired in the early evening. See the units ready reckoner for more information on calculating how much you have drunk.

Long-term effects and alcohol-related illnesses

Alcohol is a poisonous substance so having it frequently circulating in your body will harm your health. Regular drinking may damage internal organs even if you rarely drink to the point of intoxication. Several serious diseases occur more frequently in heavy drinkers than in the rest of the population. It is however fair to point out that most of the problems listed below (with the exception of liver cirrhosis) are not caused by drinking alcohol alone. Unlike cigarette smoking, which directly causes most cases of lung cancer, alcohol increases the risk of developing certain diseases, rather than being the only cause. It can also make some conditions worse. Alcohol's role in ill health is often under-recognised – doctors do not routinely ask patients how much they drink, even in cases where drinking is known to be a key factor.

Research shows excessive drinking can damage most organs and body systems:

- *Brain* – heavy drinkers suffer brain shrinkage (loss of brain cells) and even moderate drinking may effect brain function.

- *Stomach* – alcohol is a common cause of gastritis and stomach bleeding.

- *Blood and heart* – alcohol is an important cause of high blood pressure (hypertension), itself a cause of stroke.

- *Liver* – heavy drinking can cause fatty deposits in the liver, eventually leading to cirrhosis. A liver damaged by alcohol cannot process the nutrients in food, nor eliminate toxins from the blood.

- *Cancer* – excessive drinking doubles the risk of cancer of the gullet, trebles the risk of cancer of the throat and quadruples the risk of cancer of the voice box. There is evidence that it can increase the risk of breast cancer:

- *Nervous system* – nerve pains or tightening in the arms and legs can be caused by drinking large amounts.

- *Other problems* – vitamin deficiency, obesity, sexual difficulties and infertility, muscle disease, skin problems and pancreatitis have all been linked to excess alcohol consumption.

- *For women* – women are more susceptible to some of the long-term effects of alcohol, and can develop liver disease at lower levels of drinking than men.

- *Pregnancy* – there has been considerable concern about the effect of alcohol on the developing child. Some babies born to women who drink heavily in pregnancy have a condition known as Foetal Alcohol Syndrome (FAS) – a combination of growth deficiencies, central nervous system defects, lowered IQ and facial malformations. Research has shown that FAS is

found in about one-third of babies where the mother has drunk more than 56 units of alcohol a week throughout her pregnancy. Some research has identified FAS among babies of women drinking between 35 and 42 units a week. There is very little evidence to suggest a single heavy drinking bout causes any harm to the unborn baby.

Some evidence suggests that women drinking more than 10 units a week are more likely to have underweight babies. It is not clear if there is a totally safe limit for alcohol intake in pregnancy. However it is generally agreed that 1 drink a day presents a very low risk.

- *Mental health* – despite initially helping to relieve tension, alcohol can actually heighten anxiety. It is a factor in many cases of depression too, and it is estimated that alcohol has been involved in about 65% of suicide attempts.

- *Dependency* – taken often and in large quantities, alcohol is addictive – that is a person needs to drink to prevent unpleasant and occasionally dangerous withdrawal symptoms.

New advice on sensible drinking

The sensible drinking guidance has in recent years been for men to drink no more than 21 units, and women no more than 14 units, a week. It is now considered more helpful to view this guidance in daily terms and is therefore recommended that men should drink no more than three to four units a day and women no more than two to three units a day.

Men consistently drinking four units a day and women consistently drinking three units a day incur a progressive health risk.

A unit of alcohol is equivalent to:
half a pint of average-strength beer
or
a glass of wine
or
a standard pub measure of spirits
or
fortified wine such as sherry or port

© *Alcohol Concern*

Student's guide to Alcoholics Anonymous (AA)

What should you learn about alcoholism and AA?

Alcoholism is recognised as a major health problem. In the US and the UK it is the third great killer after heart disease and cancer – and it does not damage alcoholics alone. Others are hurt by its effects – in the home, at work and on the road. Alcoholism costs the community millions of pounds every year. So whether or not you ever become an alcoholic yourself, alcoholism still can have an impact on your life.

We have learned a great deal about how to identify and arrest alcoholism. But so far no one has discovered a way to prevent it, because nobody knows exactly *why* some drinkers turn into alcoholics. Doctors and scientists in the field have not agreed on the cause (or causes) of alcoholism.

For that reason, AA concentrates on helping those that are already alcoholics, so that they can stop drinking and learn how to live a normal, happy life without alcohol.

What is alcoholism?

As AA sees it, alcoholism is an illness. The alcoholic cannot control his drinking because he is ill in his body and in his mind (or emotions), AA believes. If he does not stop drinking, his alcoholism almost always gets worse and worse.

Both the American Medical Association and the British Medical Association, chief organisations of doctors in those countries, also have said that alcoholism is an illness.

What are the symptoms?

Not all alcoholics have the same symptoms, but many – at different stages in the illness – show these signs: they find that only alcohol can make them feel self-confident and at ease with other people; often want 'just one more' at the end of a party; look forward to drinking occasions and think about them a lot; get drunk when they had not planned to; try to control their drinking by changing types of liquor, going on the wagon or taking pledges; sneak drinks; lie about their drinking; hide bottles; drink at work (or in school); drink alone; have blackouts (that is, cannot remember the next day what they said or did the night before); drink in the morning to cure severe hangovers, guilty feelings and fears; fail to eat and become malnourished; get cirrhosis of the liver; shake violently, hallucinate or have convulsions when withdrawn from alcohol.

What is AA?

Alcoholics Anonymous is a worldwide fellowship of men and women who help each other to stay sober. They offer the same help to anyone who has a drinking problem and wants to do something about it. Since they are all alcoholics themselves, they have a special understanding of each other. They know what the illness feels like – and they have learned how to recover from it in AA.

An AA member says, 'I *am* an alcoholic' – even when he has not had a drink for many years. He does not say that he is 'cured'. Once a person has lost the ability to control his drinking, this AA would explain, he can never again manage a drink safely – or, in other words, he can never become 'a former alcoholic' or 'an ex- alcoholic'. But in AA he can become a sober alcoholic, a recovered alcoholic.

How does AA help the alcoholic?

Through the example and friendship of the recovered alcoholics in AA, the new member is encouraged to stay away from a drink 'one day at a time' as they do. Instead of 'swearing off forever' or worrying about whether he will be sober tomorrow, the alcoholic concentrates on not drinking right now – today.

By keeping alcohol out of his system, the newcomer takes care of one part of his illness – his body has a chance to get well. But remember, there is another part. If he is going to *stay* sober, he needs a healthy mind

and healthy emotions, too. So he begins to straighten out his confused thinking and unhappy feelings by following AA's 'Twelve Steps' to recovery. These Steps *suggest* ideas and actions that can guide him towards a happy and useful life.

To be in touch with other members and to learn about the recovery programme, the new member goes to AA meetings regularly.

What are AA meetings?

Alcoholics Anonymous is made up of about 65,000 local groups, in 100 countries. In Great Britain and the Channel Islands there are more than 2,200 local groups. The people in each group get together, usually once or twice a week, to hold AA meetings, of two main types.

1. At 'open' meetings, speakers tell how they drank, how they discovered AA and how its programme has helped them. Members may bring relatives or friends and usually anyone interested in AA is also welcome to attend 'open' meetings.
2. 'Closed' meetings are for alcoholics only. These are group discussions, and any member who wants to may speak up, to ask questions and to share his thoughts with his fellow members. At 'closed' meetings, each AA can help with his personal problems in staying sober and in everyday living. Some other AA will have had the same problems and can explain how he handled them – often by using one or more of the Twelve Steps.

Who belongs to AA?

Like other illnesses, alcoholism strikes all sorts of people. So the men and women in AA are of all races and nationalities, all religions and no religion at all. They are rich and poor and just average. They work at all occupations, as lawyers and housewives, teachers and truck drivers, waitresses and clergymen.

AA does not keep a list of members, but groups do report how many people belong to each one. From these reports, the total membership of AA is estimated at over one and a half million.

Does an alcoholic have to go 'all the way down' before AA can help him?

AA was started in 1935 by a New York stockbroker and an Ohio surgeon who had both been 'hopeless' drunks. The first group in England started in early 1947. At first, most AA members also had been seriously ill; their drinking had sent them to hospitals, sanatoriums or jails. But more and more people began to hear about AA and soon many alcoholics found they did not have to let their illness do that much damage. They could recover in AA *before* their health had been totally wrecked, while they still had their jobs and their families.

Are there any young people in AA?

In recent years, a great many young alcoholics have come into AA. The pamphlet *Young People and AA* gives the personal stories of ten who joined when they were under 30 – including one who joined at 18, one at 16. These young people are cheerfully staying sober and taking part in AA activities.

Who runs AA?

AA has no real government. Each group is free to work out its own customs and ways of holding meetings as long as it does not hurt other groups or AA as a whole. The members elect a chairman, a secretary and other group officers. These officers do not give orders to anybody; mostly, their job is to see that the meetings run smoothly. In the average group, new officers are elected twice a year.

But the individual group is not cut off from the rest of AA. Just as AA members help each other, so do AA groups. Here are three of the means they use to exchange help:

1. Groups in the same area set up a central office or 'Intergroup' office.
2. Groups share their experiences by writing to the AA General Service Office in York.
3. Groups in Great Britain and the Channel Islands choose representatives to go to the AA General Service Conference, held once a year.

All these AA offices and the representatives at the Conferences make *suggestions*, based on the experiences of many different AA groups. But they do not make rules or issue commands to any groups or members.

What does it cost to belong to AA?

Newcomers do not pay any fees for membership. And members do not pay dues.

But money *is* needed for some AA purposes: renting the meeting hall, buying coffee and other refreshments, buying AA books, pamphlets and magazines. So a basket is usually passed around during the meeting and members put in whatever they can afford or wish to give. Groups also contribute money to support central offices, the General Service Office and other AA activities.

In return for the AA help that members give to other alcoholics, these members are never paid. Their reward is something much better than money – it is their own health. AAs have found that helping other alcoholics is the best way to stay sober themselves.

What can the families of alcoholics do?

AA is just for the alcoholics, but two other fellowships can help their relatives. One is Al-Anon Family Groups. The other is Alateen, for teenagers who have alcoholic parents.

What does AA *not* do?

1. AA does *not* run membership drives to try to argue alcoholics into joining. AA is for alcoholics who *want* to get sober.
2. AA does *not* check up on its members to see that they don't drink. It helps alcoholics to help *themselves*.
3. AA is *not* a religious organisation. Each member is free to decide his own personal ideas about the meaning of life.
4. AA is *not* a medical organisation, does *not* give out medicines or psychiatric advice.
5. AA does *not* run any hospitals, wards or sanatoriums or provide nursing services.

6. AA is *not* connected with any other organisation. But AA does co-operate with organisations that fight alcoholism. Some members work for such organisations – but on their own – *not* as representatives of AA.
7. AA does *not* accept money from sources outside AA, either private or government.
8. AA does *not* offer any social services, does *not* provide housing, food, clothing, jobs or money. It helps the alcoholic stay sober, so he can earn these things for himself.
9. Alcoholics Anonymous lives up to the 'Anonymous' part of its title. It does *not* want members' names to be told on TV or radio or in newspapers. And members do not tell other members' names to people outside AA. But members are *not* ashamed of belonging to AA. They just want

to encourage more alcoholics to come to AA for help. And they do *not* want to make heroes and heroines of themselves simply for taking care of their own health.

How can you find out more about AA?

1. Most towns and cities have an AA listing in the telephone book, for a group or central office. Often, local AA has a public information committee to tell people what they want to know about AA.
2. If you do not find an AA listing in your phone book, write to: AA General Service Office, PO Box 1, Stonebow House, Stonebow, York YO1 2NJ.
3. You can get other AA pamphlets by writing to the General Service Office (address above).
4. In local libraries, you may find copies of these AA books: *Alcoholics Anonymous*, *Alcoholics Anonymous Comes of Age*, *The Twelve Steps and Twelve Traditions*, *AA Way of Life* (new title – *As Bill Sees It*)
5. The AA monthly magazine *SHARE* may be obtained from your local AA group or by writing for information to: 'SHARE', PO Box 1, Stonebow House, Stonebow, York YO1 2NJ.

© *Alcoholics Anonymous*

Worried about someone else?

Information from Alcohol Concern

How to tell if someone else has a problem with alcohol

For those worried about someone else's drinking a common question is – are they actually alcoholic? The problem is that most people with a drinking problem will deny it. The question is usually paramount in the minds of those concerned because finding out by other means is difficult. The person (who is unlikely to appear completely drunk) will be resistant to any enquiries, is likely to lie about their drinking and will take a lot of trouble to cover it up. You know something is wrong and suspect alcohol, but because of the stigma attached to alcohol problems which contributes to denial (often aggressive), it is hard to find out from the person directly. In fact the question itself is rarely very useful, unless the person is willing to talk about their drinking, and when thinking about what action needs to be taken. It is likely that if you are concerned about someone and think drink is involved

then it probably is. It is more useful to focus on what has changed rather than whether or not someone is 'alcoholic'.

Some signs of a drink problem are:

A) Changes in mood and behaviour
You may start to notice a person's moods change more quickly and erratically. It can be quite hard to define, but these changes in temperament do not appear to have a logical basis. You may feel uneasy when you are with the person, as if something is 'going on' that you are not fully aware of. Changes in mood and behaviour can manifest in many ways. Some examples you may notice are, in group conversations people with a developing drink problem may have difficulty concentrating on the topic under discussion. They appear distracted for a while then suddenly join in with an unrelated remark or comment, or just respond inappropriately. They usually appear unaware

of, or just simply ignore any signs of discomfort shown by others at their behaviour. The drinker is probably conscious of being distracted, and overcompensates causing puzzlement in others. Obviously this may happen if people have other problems on their minds or are unwell. Also, the degree to which it is noticeable varies according to an individual's personality – in a quiet person it would be less noticeable than in a more lively character. How well you know them and the level and nature of contact you have also has a bearing. What is important is if this is a new behaviour and if the person appears to be unaware of the unease caused to others by their attempt to cover up and appear 'normal'.

Perhaps more definite are memory lapses or confusion about recent conversations and events. People with a drink problem may repeat recent conversations, not remembering that the issue has already been discussed, and rather than just admit they have forgotten, they will attempt to cover up. More disturbing can be the person who has been argumentative, but having forgotten the dispute, may appear to blame you for any tension.

Becoming increasingly un-reliable at work or at home with jobs and responsibilities that they used to handle well, is common in people with alcohol problems. They can become increasingly defensive if tackled about this, blaming circum-stances and other people for things not running smoothly.

An increasing lack of awareness of wider events is often evident as the problem drinker either just loses interest in outside events or is too preoccupied to take notice of them.

B) Changes in drinking patterns
It may be obvious that someone's drinking pattern has changed. They may be going out much more often to drink, or drinking at home or alone when they didn't before. They may switch to stronger drinks – from beer to spirits for example. They may start drinking at earlier times during the day. You may be aware of them spending more on drink than they can really afford.

A person with a drink problem may start to lie about their move-ments – say they have been held up at work when really they have been to the pub. You may be able to smell drink on their breath at inappropriate times or when the person denies having had a drink. You may catch them drinking secretly. They may frequently disappear for short periods of time to top up. You may find alcohol in odd places – at home, in bedrooms and cupboards – or at work. Empties may be suddenly thrown directly into the dustbin rather than the kitchen waste bin.

C) Physical signs
At some stage a reduction in the care of personal appearance and hygiene is common in people with alcohol problems. Perhaps you notice a deterioration in the home, meals, garden or other things that the person used to care about. There will be physical deterioration and increas-ingly frequent bouts of ill-health, which the drinker is unlikely to attribute to their drinking. They may tremble and sweat at certain times, and be quite flushed. Vomiting is common in the morning. People with drink problems bruise easily as a result of vitamin deficiencies and therefore the signs of falls or knocks are often apparent. There is a lack of physical co-ordination generally. You might be aware of their black-outs, their anxiety and depression, poor appetite and insomnia.

Finding help
People often don't know how best to help someone with a drink problem.

If you are close to a problem drinker it can be hard because you and your family may be having to put up with the difficult behaviour whilst the drinker does not recognise or admit they have a problem. Even when they do, it can be very difficult for them to stop drinking or cut down and this in itself is a source of tension for their partners and friends. How you approach the problem and respond to it is important, but it may have got beyond the resources of the people involved leading to distress and guilt as the family and friends try, but fail to help.

The wisest thing to do in these circumstances, is to get some independent advice and support, even if this is to just check out whether your suspicions are accurate.

Advice and counselling agen-cies exist throughout the country and the staff are more than happy to talk to friends and family members either on the phone or by appointment. They can support you, help you make decisions about what you want to do, and importantly, if you feel you can continue to help the drinker, they can offer guidance on ways that are more likely to have an effect. Talking to others in the same situation helps a lot of people and self-help groups do exist for families, friends and partners of problem drinkers. Drink-ing problems are a lot more common than you may think.

The Alcohol Services Directory section, on the Alcohol Concern web site, will tell you where your nearest alcohol advice agency is. Check to see if there is one in your nearest town by looking in the section for your county or metro-politan borough.

Also check your local phone book under Alcohol. The Drinkline National Alcohol Helpline number for information on local agencies is 0171-332-0202 (London area only) and 0345-32-02-02 (rest of UK, charged at local rates). You can find out about self-help groups in your area by contacting Al-Anon on 0171-403-0888. See page 41 for address details and page 43 for web site details. © *Alcohol Concern*

When a parent drinks too much

Information from the Scottish Council on Alcohol

When someone has a drinking problem, they're not the only one who suffers. Heavy drinking affects friends and family and often makes them as unhappy as the drinker.

People who have a drink problem may let drink control their lives. They may forget the feelings of the people who are close to them. They may not realise that their drinking is upsetting the family.

How do you cope?

If one of your parents has a drinking problem, you will find it hard to cope.

- you may feel scared, panicky, confused, mixed-up.
- you will wonder 'what's going to happen next?'
- you will be angry and upset at the drinker's way of behaving especially when you are let down or have promises broken.
- you could feel helpless and angry at yourself because you can't change things.
- worst of all you may even feel guilty that somehow you are to blame – you are not to blame.

It's hard to cope with all these bad feelings and you might find it difficult to think straight. Maybe you try to keep things going at home by doing things yourself that otherwise wouldn't get done, like housework, shopping, looking after brothers or sisters even if this means taking time off school or work.

Perhaps you have tried to protect the drinker by hiding things from relatives and neighbours and even employers. You may have pretended to yourself that the problem doesn't really exist or will soon go away. Through all this, you will probably have started to feel very lonely and different from your friends and other people your age. Perhaps you feel you no longer have a life of your own. Even the parent who doesn't have a drink problem may seem to nag you all the time.

What can you do?

The most important thing to do is to work out a way of keeping things going as normally as possible.

Someone with a drink problem can't change their ways very quickly so you may have to live with the problem for a long time. Try and come to terms with that as soon as you can and minimise the problem being caused.

Don't try to lecture the drinker, especially when they have been drinking. There may be times when it will be possible to talk to them in an easy, friendly way, about their drinking and what it's doing to the family and how it upsets you.

This might make them feel it is time to get help. Try to be helpful to your other parent who may have all sorts of problems to deal with too because of their partner's drinking.

First – find out about alcohol

- Learn as much as you can.
- Go and see someone at an Advice Centre dealing with alcohol problems.
- There is a book that you can buy called *Living with a drinker*.
- Don't try to cope by drinking yourself. It won't help with the problems you already have and could cause you many more.

Next – talk to someone you trust

- people who really care for you
- friends, relatives, teachers or neighbours.

Then – learn not to blame yourself

- you are not responsible for the problems in the family.
- don't think that your parents do bad things because of you, or because they don't love you.
- don't allow them to expect things of you because you feel sorry for them, either.

You know when it's wrong for a grown-up to do or ask certain things of you. If you are asked to keep a special secret or to do something you feel is wrong, that's the time to tell a responsible adult.

For help or further information contact

The Scottish Council on Alcohol, 2nd Floor, 166 Buchanan Street, Glasgow G1 2NH. Telephone: 0141 333 9677 Fax: 0141 333 1606, e-mail: SCA@clara. net or your local alcohol agency.

© Scottish Council on Alcohol

ADDITIONAL RESOURCES

You might like to contact the following organisations for further information. Due to the increasing cost of postage, many organisations cannot respond to enquiries unless they receive a stamped, addressed envelope.

Al-Anon Family Groups UK and Eire (AFG)
61 Great Dover Street
London, SE1 4YF
Tel: 0171 403 0888
Helps families of problem drinkers. Alateen, part of Al-Anon, helps teenagers who have been, or who are, affected by an alcoholic relative. Publishes a wide selection of leaflets and books.

Alcohol Concern
Waterbridge House
32-36 Loman Street
London, SE1 0EE
Tel: 0171 928 7377
Fax: 0171 928 4644
Works with the Government, statutory and other voluntary bodies. Alcohol Concern aims to develop more and better treatment services nationally, to increase public and professional awareness of alcohol misuse and to bring about a reduction in alcohol-related problems. They produce a wide range of factsheets and other publications.

Alcoholics Anonymous (AA)
General Service Office
PO Box 1, Stonebow House
Stonebow
York, YO1 2NJ
Tel: 01904 644026
A fellowship of men and women who share their experience, strength and hope with each other that they may solve their common problem and help others to recover from alcoholism. Ask for their publications list.

Campaign Against Drinking and Driving (CADD)
83 Jesmond Road
Newcastle upon Tyne, NE2 1NH
Tel: 0191 281 1581
Fax: 0191 281 4591
Supports and assists the victims and families of victims who have suffered death or injury by drunken drivers on the roads in the UK.

Health Education Authority
Trevelyan House
30 Great Peter Street
London, SW1P 2HW
Tel: 0171 222 5300
Fax: 0171 413 8900
The Health Education Authority is a special health authority within the NHS and has a statutory responsibility to advise the Government on health education issues. It is the national centre of excellence for health education research and expertise and, through its campaigns, publications and work with health professionals, encourages the public to adopt healthier lifestyles.

Institute for the Study of Drug Dependency (ISDD)
Waterbridge House
32-36 Loman Street
London, SE1 0EE
Tel: 0171 928 1211
Fax: 0171 928 1771
Disseminates information and promote research on all aspects of drug misuse.

Institute of Alcohol Studies (IAS)
Alliance House
12 Caxton Street
London, SW1H 0QS
Tel: 0171 222 4001
Fax: 0171 222 2510
Produces a wide range of factsheets, posters, papers and books on alcohol-related issues.

Lifeline
101-103 Oldham Street
Manchester, M4 1LW
Tel: 0161 839 2054
Fax: 0161 834 5903

National Council for Social Concern
Montague Chambers
Montague Close
London, SE1 9DA
Tel: 0171 403 0977
Fax: 0171 403 0799

Promotes the restoration to the community of ex-offenders and of people addicted to alcohol, drugs or gambling. Produces publications.

Schools Health Education Unit
Renslade House
Bonhay Road
Exeter, EX4 3AY
Tel: 01392 667272
Fax: 01392 667269
Publish *Young People and Alcohol: its use and abuse*, priced at £17.00.

TACADE (Advisory Council on Alcohol and Drug Education)
1 Hulme Place
The Crescent
Salford
Greater Manchester, M5 4QA
Tel: 0161 745 8925
Fax: 0161 745 8923
Works in the field of preventative education. Publishes a wide range of factsheets on drug-related issues in their *Basic Facts* series.

The Portman Group
2d Wimpole Street
London, W1M 7AA
Tel: 0171 499 1010
Fax: 0171 493 1417
Established by the eight leading UK drinks companies to: promote sensible drinking; reduce alcohol-related harm; and develop a better understanding of alcohol misuse.

The Scottish Council on Alcohol (SCA)
2nd Floor
166 Buchanan Street
Glasgow, G1 2NH
Tel: 0141 333 9677
Fax: 0141 333 1606

Welsh Drug and Alcohol Unit (WDAU)
4th Floor, St David's House
Wood Street
Cardiff, CF1 1EY
Tel: 01222 667766
Fax: 01222 665940

INDEX

Independence Web News

Back | Forward | Home | Reload | Images | Open | Print | Find | Stop

Live Home Page | Search | Computer | Support | System

The Internet has been likened to shopping in a supermarket without aisles. The press of a button on a Web browser can bring up thousands of sites but working your way through them to find what you want can involve long and frustrating on-line searches. And unfortunately many sites contain inaccurate, misleading or heavily biased information. Our researchers have therefore undertaken an extensive analysis to bring you a selection of quality Web site addresses.

* * * * *

Alcohol Concern
www.alcoholconcern.org.uk
A huge site with factsheets, news and links to other relevant sites.

Alcoholics Anonymous (AA)
www.recovery.org/aa
Online AA Recovery Resources: a large collection of Alcoholics Anonymous information.

Institute of Alcohol Studies
www.ias.org.uk
Looking for general information on alcohol? Need factsheets? Press releases? Then this is a very useful starting-point.

Patient Information Publications
www.patient.org.uk/addict
Provides UK self-help and patient groups web links.

The National Association for Children of Alcoholics
www.health.org/nacoa
A very US-oriented site but it contains quite useful information.

The National Institute on Alcohol Abuse and Alcoholism (NIAAA)
www.niaaa.nih.gov
Has a useful section on frequently asked questions on alcohol and alcoholism.

The Web of Addictions
www.well.com/user/woa
The Web of Addictions is dedicated to providing accurate information about alcohol and other drug addictions.

Wrecked
www.wrecked.co.uk
Not a lot of information but it does offer brief insights.

ACKNOWLEDGEMENTS

The publisher is grateful for permission to reproduce the following material.

While every care has been taken to trace and acknowledge copyright, the publisher tenders its apology for any accidental infringement or where copyright has proved untraceable. The publisher would be pleased to come to a suitable arrangement in any such case with the rightful owner.

Chapter One: The Impact of Alcohol

Alcohol, © Institute for the Study of Drug Dependency (ISDD), *Sensible drinking*, © General Household Survey, HMSO, *Alcohol and the law*, © Alcohol Concern, *Facts about alcohol*, © Lifeline, *Intoxicating facts*, © Health Education Authority (HEA), *Booze: Britain's real drug crisis*, © The Independent, August 1998, *Weekly alcohol consumption levels*, © General Household Survey, Crown copyright is reproduced with the permission of the Controller of Her Majesty's Stationery Office (HMSO), *Alcohol problems and work statistics*, © Alcohol Concern, *Social costs of alcohol*, © Alcohol Concern, *What too much drink does to you*, © The Daily Mail, September 1998, *20 questions on sensible drinking*, © The Portman Group, March 1998, *Too much drink?*, © Health Education Authority (HEA), 1998, *Alcohol summary facts*, © Health Education Authority (HEA), 1998, *Too much teen spirit*, © The Independent, June 1998, *Type of drinks*, © Health in England 1996, HMSO, *Alcopops – no soft options*, © Young People Now, September 1997, *Alcohol 'soft' drinks*, © Health in England 1996, Crown copyright is reproduced with the permission of the Controller of Her Majesty's Stationery Office (HMSO), *11-year-olds get drinking habit with 'alcopops'*, © Telegraph Group Limited, May 1997, *Alcopops 'not to blame for luring the young'*, © Telegraph Group Limited, London 1997, *It all adds up*, © The Portman Group, March 1998, *The sensible drinking quiz*, © The Portman Group, March 1998, *Under the influence*, © Alcohol Concern, *Weekly consumption*, © Health in England 1996, Crown copyright is reproduced with the permission of the Controller of Her Majesty's Stationery Office (HMSO), *Could red wine really do more good than harm?*, © The Daily Mail, April 1997, *Drink and be damned*, The Guardian, August 1998, *Condon links drink to rise in violence*, © The Independent, June 1998, *Doctors dispute drop in drink-related violence*, © The Scotsman, January 1998, *Move to reduce alcohol limit in drive to cut road deaths*, © The Independent, January 1998, *Cost of exceeding the limit*, © The Portman Group, *Ignorance over drink levels*, © The Guardian, December 1997, *Drinking and driving*, © Department of the Environment, Transport and the Regions, Crown copyright is reproduced with the permission of the Controller of Her Majesty's Stationery Office (HMSO), *Alcohol tops problems in casualty*, © The Guardian, March 1998, *Drinking and driving*, © Department of the Environment, Transport and the Regions, Crown copyright is reproduced with the permission of the Controller of Her Majesty's Stationery Office (HMSO), *Drink-drive plan is shelved as EU stops interfering*, © Telegraph Group Limited, London 1998, *Drink-driving limits in the EU*, © EU, *Drink-drive payout could reach £3m*, © The Independent, June 1998, *Police enforcement*, © Department of the Environment, Transport and the Regions, Crown copyright is reproduced with the permission of the Controller of Her Majesty's Stationery Office (HMSO).

Chapter Two: Seeking Help

Do I have an alcohol problem?, © Alcohol Concern, *Help for alcohol problems*, © Alcohol Concern, *Students guide to Alcoholics Anonymous (AA)*, © Alcoholics Anonymous, *Worried about someone else?*, © Alcohol Concern, *When a parent drinks too much*, © Scottish Council on Alcohol (SCA).

Photographs and illustrations:

Pages 1, 2, 5, 9, 22, 26, 33, 39: Pumpkin House, pages 11, 25, 27: Ken Pyne, page 13: Katherine Fleming, page 36: Andrew Smith.

Craig Donnellan
Cambridge
January, 1999